THE ART
of
SCREENWRITING

Simplified

THE ART
of
SCREENWRITING
Simplified

The Most Comprehensive Guide for Film and Television

Written and Compiled by
W.E.N. Screenwriters & Associates

BAWN Publishers Inc.
Cincinnati, Ohio

THE ART OF SCREENWRITING *Simplified*

W.E.N. Screenwriters & Associates

BAWN Publishers Inc.

P.O. Box 15965

Cincinnati, Ohio 45215-0965

Copyright © 1995 by W.E.N. Screenwriters & Associates

Copyeditor:	Beverly Nason
Cover Design:	BAWN Publishers Inc.
Interior Design:	W.E.N. Screenwriters & Associates
Production:	BAWN Publishers Inc.

Distribution

BAWN Publishers books are distributed by BAWN Publishers, P.O. Box 15965, Cincinnati, Ohio 45215-0965.

Acknowledgements

Acknowledgements are made to the following: *Making a Good Script Great* by Linda Segar, Dodd Mead; *Writing the Script*, Wells Roots Holt, Rinehart & Winston; *The Screenwriters Handbook* , W.E.N. Screenwriters & Assoc.; *Creating Unforgettable Characters*, Linda Segar, Henry Holt and Company, Inc.; *The Screenwriter's Bible* , David Trottier, The Screenwriting Center.

This book is dedicated to all those who have a story to tell. With all things considered and being equal and as you follow this manual in conjunction with other materials you may have or will read, we hope your understanding of screenwriting will be enlightened.

Table of Contents

Preface

Section One

Section Two

Section Three

Section Four

Section Five

PREFACE

The making of a good script or screenplay takes a combination of various skills. These are skills which each and every person possess in some form. The only problem is, most people are unaware that they have the necessary skills. To be a writer, one must have a fresh approach or a different look at the subject he/she is about to write. This approach has to be original, unique, creative in style and in proper format. You will need to have a sense of what might appeal to people and KNOW HOW TO TELL A GOOD STORY.

Most important of all, you need to know how to structure and how to execute the story so that it makes sense. In 99% of the majority of cases, most producers, story editors, directors and studio executives find the same problem with new writers. They criticize structure problems, unclear storylines, poorly motivated characters, rambling subplots, too many characters, endings that don't fit the beginnings and too many unanswered questions at the end. (We understand that many of the terms and/or phrases just used makes no sense, but all of them will be discussed in detail throughout this manual.) As you can see, the list of potential problems that can arise with new writers seem endless. The majority of new writers somehow overlook one additional and probably one of the most important and relevant parts of writing their scripts, *proper format*. The formats for TV and Motion pictures, are similar in many ways but different in others. ALL of the above mentioned problems are reparable in the rewriting stages. Yes, I said that dreadful word *rewriting*. The rewriting stage is considered one of the most dreadful, boring and tedious parts of the writing process. But, keep in mind, as dreadful, boring and tedious as it may seem, it is one of the most important stages in the scriptwriting process.

Before you read this manual, you may think that your ideas for a new movie, TV show or episode of an existing show is a sheer work of art. And you should. But when you begin the rewriting process, you should approach your script in a more analytical way. To put it simply, look at it and break it down to make sure your thoughts are both magical and creative, yet in an established style. What we have tried to do in this manual is discuss the underlying concepts that make a workable, well written and more cohesive script. These elements are extremely important parts of creating a great screenplay whether you are new at writing or experienced.

Working with these elements can make your first draft easier and the rewrites just as easy, leading to a stronger, more integrated script and later film. There are a lot of good scripts, but the trick is not to write just a *good* script, but the challenge is turning a *good* script into a *great* script. That is your goal. It's the process where the art of creative writing creates the MAGIC of film.

We hope that after reading this manual, you have more control, better insight and a better understanding into how to put a workable and marketable screenplay together. Anyone—yes anyone, can learn to write a professional screenplay. When given the right tools and information, all you need is an idea of what you want to say. This manual was compiled and written to give you all the tools and information you will need to bring that idea to life.

Section One

Screenwriting Fundamentals

Outline

Creating Characters

Character Functions

The Setup

Summary

Screenwriting Fundamentals

In this Section, we will discuss the basic information necessary to begin your journey toward completion of your first, and hopefully many more screenplays. This section will guide you through the maze of thoughts which will flood your mind. It may, as well dispel some preconceived notions about how a movie is made and put you on the right track.

Section One

OUTLINE

The *outline* is the process which is used to layout your story. You should, in three to five pages, be able to tell your entire story from beginning to end with exceptions of dialogue, stage direction, camera cues and angles etc.

In the film and TV industry, outline also refers to what is commonly called a *treatment* or *synopsis*. They are all one in the same. If at any time during your reading of the manual, either of the terms—outline, treatment or synopsis is used, they all mean the exact same thing.

The outline must bring together all of the following vital information:

- style (comedy, drama, action adventure, etc.)

- theme of the story (what the story is about)

- main characters

- main characters' backgrounds

- any unique characteristics (mannerisms) of the characters

- locations and time changes

Describing all of the above elements in your outline will help move your story toward its *climax*.

The outline, as well as your script, must be laid out in a three act format—beginning, middle and end. These three elements are essential to each and every story because without them no story can or will exist.

(See examples in Section Five, **sample treatments**). Use the examples as your reference in developing your own outline. The outline will keep you, your story as well as characters on track. And, you won't waste valuable time as you proceed.

CREATING CHARACTERS

Character development is essential to writing a great story. A character that is well-developed in your story is created by the various encounters they face throughout the story. Your characters should be **unforgettable**.

There are keys to creating unforgettable characters. These keys, further defined below, are vital and apply to main characters as well as supporting and minor characters.

The keys are:

Motivation

Dimensional Characters

Goal and Opposition

The following are a few good examples that you can use as a guide in developing your characters.

Motivation

Motivation is the emotional touch between the audience and your character. As you develop your character, ask yourself: why does my main character want what she/he wants? What keeps them going? This is *motivation*—the more personal, the better. In fact, the more personal, the more the audience will identify and/or empathize with your character.

In *Rocky*, Rocky's main goal was to go 15 rounds with the champ. Why? To prove he was not a bum! It's the personal motivation that gives the story power.

In *Rocky 2*, Rocky's wife goes into a coma. Then she blinks and opens her eyes and says "Win!" Now Rocky has a motive for winning.

In *Rainman*, Tom Cruises's perception of his father's past harsh treatment of him drives him toward his goal of collecting the inheritance. In other words, he wants the inheritance to get back at his father.

Dimensional Characters

Dimensional characters have values, emotions, attitudes and inconsistencies.

When you judge a person, do you judge them by their words or actions? More times than not, we tend to judge their actions rather than words. These same tendencies should also apply in developing our characters.

Make your characters more alive by emphasizing actions. In some circumstances, a character's words might play more of a role than their actions, i.e., in a court case, where not only actions but words as well are used. Develop your character's actions so that their "true colors" are revealed. A person's actions are a direct result of who she/he is. Give the character problems and/or obstacles and let them reveal their true nature by how they handle these problems.

In *Philadelphia*, Joe Miller changed the direction of the story when he decided to take Andrew Beckett's case. He was moved with compassion only after seeing Andrew undergo a discriminatory act at the library.

There are similar relationships between character and story with Edna in *Places in the Heart* and Matt and Martin in *Jaws*.

Each of these main characters entered the story as dimensional and stereotypical. Each became more dimensional as the story and other characters impacted upon them by advising, teaching, fighting, confronting, pressuring and influencing them. Because they were created **bigger than life**, they were able to be further developed due to the impact provided by the other characters. This helped to make the main characters more believable as they changed.

Some characters are only one dimensional and are defined by their physical appearance such as: a balding professor, a macho detective or a muscle-bound lifeguard, etc. These type of characters have only small roles and act as window dressing for the set.

On occasion there are main characters who limit the film by their limited dimensions. For example, in what is considered a grade C or D or a low budget film, the main characters have limited acting ability and/or dialogue. But a well-developed character is broader and more fleshed out. Meaning, you can see the different side, understand how they think as they act , as well as be aware of their emotional makeup through their response. We call this a three dimensional character, which consists of thoughts, actions, and emotions.

A Goal and Opposition

As a character moves from motivation to goal, something must happen along the way. There must be a goal to which your character aspires. Dealing with life is not a goal. Happiness is not a goal. A search for $15 million in gold treasure from a sunken ship is a goal.

In the *Wizard of Oz*, Dorothy retrieving the broomstick from the wicked witch for the Wizard in order to return to Kansas, is a goal.

The *goal* should reveal a lot about your character. Whatever the goal, it should not be easily attained.

There must be *opposition* to your character attaining his/her goal. Opposition creates conflict which makes drama. This opposition should be an individual not an event or organization. However, if an event or organization is the opposition, let it be represented by an individual.

Example: In *Ghostbusters*, the Environmental Protection Agency is represented by a man and he makes it his personal business to close down the Ghostbusters.

Where a group of people oppose the main character such as a gang, focus on one person— the leader, i.e., the antagonist in the group. This character should be the greatest threat to the main character. It is possible to have a nonhuman opposition, such as in *Jaws*, a great white shark.

TIP

As the saying goes, "Actions speak louder than words". Your character needs to reveal as much as possible through their actions, rather than dialogue.

Character Types

A *character type* is a character who can be defined by only one category. James Bond is a character type. He's a hero and identified only by his actions. All we know is that he likes to sleep with beautiful women. His emotional life is totally irrelevant and nonexistent. We never see him cry or show fear, insecurity, or anger or be anything else but cool. These type of characters may seem to portray the perfect person, but their casting roles are limited.

Well-developed characters can be further divided into three parts:

Thinking consists of a character's philosophy and attitudes.

Acting consists of the actions as well as decisions that lead to the character's responses.

Emotions include the emotional makeup of the character, as well as responses.

As in any well-developed character, one of these characteristics might be stronger. But with the addition of each of the others, they will contribute to creating that three dimensional character.

Philosophy and Attitude

Philosophy and attitude represents a belief system, with varying perceptions of reality. These perceptions influence our present by past experiences.

A point of view is developed over time. In some way our current experience filters through from our past experiences.

Two different people may experience the same stimulus, but depending on their perceptions, react totally different in expressing their attitudes.

Philosophy is the most difficult characteristic of all to portray. However, your characters need to believe in something—be it religion, gay or women's rights or God. Their actions should reflect their beliefs.

For example, if a person believes in gay rights, she/he will march, be vocal and may be a practicing homosexual. That philosophy will take form by their actions.

When characters are defined *too much* by their personal beliefs, they become abstract, talky, self-indulgent and usually quite *boring*.

Attitudes, by contrast, are much easier to portray than philosophy, whether that attitude is cynical or optimistic, happy-go-lucky, or aggressive.

All great characters will take a stance toward life in some form. The truth of a character's beliefs are far more actable and acceptable when shown through their attitudes and actions rather than their philosophy.

In creating your characters, give each character a separate set of facts based on the same *premise*, but don't give them the same view point. Then, have them act from their *point of view*, or belief system regardless if the point of view squares with reality or not.

Example:

In *Philadelphia*, Andrew Beckett is fired from his job because of aids. Andrew becomes distraught over not being able to find legal counseling, after being rejected by the tenth attorney, Joe Miller.

Joe Miller's fear of contracting aids causes him to reject Andrew's plea for help. After getting information from his doctor and being confronted by his wife regarding his fears of homosexuality, he sees Andrew in the library being confronted with more discrimination. Joe Miller is moved by compassion.

Andrew's motivation is to right a wrong by suing his former employer.

Andrew's point of view is: why should he lose his job, because of someone else's homophobia.

Joe Miller's motivation is, a discrimination law has been broken. Joe's point of view is, equal rights is for every person, not just heterosexuals only.

Andrew's disease is the *backstory*. Joe's defending Andrew is the action of the story.

Attitude is more easily expressed through action. It's not that difficult to show love, anger, compassion, receptivity or cynicism.

When or if you try to combine both philosophy and attitude, you run a dangerous risk of having the character talk this dimension, rather than act it out.

It is unfortunate but oft-times many new writers will leave out the emotional aspects of their characters. A character must have some type of an emotional makeup. Their emotions as well as their attitudes are what defines your character.

A positive attitude may result in their being always optimistic, smiling, easily accessible, and caring. Or your character may be cool as a result of a hard-core, or hostile lifestyle. This makes them inaccessible to others. Whatever the emotional makeup of the character, you as the writer have the responsibility to expand the responses.

Example: A character who is normally cool and happy, becomes angry at an injustice that's been perpetrated against someone special in their lives.

Too many films leave out the beat in the story where the character decides to take action. They also leave out the beat showing the emotional response to the action.

We often see someone get blown away, but rarely see the emotional response of the character who suffers from the death, or of the person who pulled the trigger. It's the emotional response that makes the character understandable. Emotions are what pull the audience into the story and help them identify with the character as they go along their journey.

Actions come out of the character's emotional makeup which helps them to do one thing and not another. And as a result of the actions of others, the character responds emotionally in certain ways. Combining all these responses and actions together is what builds a character.

You have successfully created your character if your character comes to the story with certain attitudes, actions and emotions and leaves changing some. When you transform a character, it can be from one extreme to another or move to a more moderate or middle of the road position. For example, a rigid, hard-nose person may have a complete transformation, becoming more spontaneous and the life of the party by the end of the story.

For your characters to change, they need help in some form. It can come from the influence of the story or another character which is the catalyst needed for the change.

It takes time to transform a character and it doesn't happen in a few pages. It normally takes the entire three acts or at least two acts to create a transformation to its opposite. So don't be in a big hurry or rush to make the character change. The beat-by-beat process is what slowly transforms them into a new person.

Have your character make a decision and then show how those decisions change throughout the story. The emotional responses to new situations, and the actions taken as they also respond to new demands placed on them, is the result of their interactions with other characters.

Decisions and Actions

Action is the lifeblood of drama. Action is divided into **two parts**: the *decision to act* and *the act itself*. As in most films, we usually see only the action.

When it's a decision to act, that action is what helps us understand how the character's mind works. A moment of decision whether or not to pull the trigger or to say yes to an assignment or to commit to a relationship, is usually a strong moment or a character's revelation. Decisions must lead to specific actions. Your characters need to be as active as possible in your story.

The job of the main character is to drive the story forward with their actions, which can be achieved in numerous ways. They can search, uncover, investigate, outwit, plan and transform others and themselves. Whatever the action, be it manipulative, vengeful or righting a wrong, it is important that they have the ability to drive the story forward.

TIP

Remember as you are developing your characters, a character's philosophy creates certain attitudes, which create decisions that create the actions.

TIP

The professional writer makes it a conscious part of their writing to move far beyond stereotypes into expanding their own understanding of people.

There are some stories where the main character starts out as passive and then something happens to push them in a certain direction in the story. At this point is when the main character has to take over the story.

Understanding Character Development

There are numerous traps and pitfalls for new writers. The task of creating dimensional characters is not easy. You should look more at everyday life for the source of your characters rather than at other films. However, it isn't entirely wrong to look at other films. But when you do make sure it's more as a learning tool. For instance, you may want to pattern one character after the attributes of another, but with a slight twist in his/her personality, etc.

Most writers tend to leave out one aspect of their characters—the character's philosophy or emotional response. Their philosophy is not as overt or easily recognizable as action. This leads writers to think the other dimensions aren't as important. Creating dimensional characters demands one to be more observant of real life. A true writer is constantly noticing small details, traits and listening for character rhythms. This gives you a deeper and broader range of thoughts, actions, emotions and responses, which gives you greater freedom.

As you begin the development of your characters, it's helpful to begin by looking at the skills and characteristics of your main characters. Then ask yourself, what will she/he need to get to the objective.

Look at where your character starts, then determine which of those characteristics will she/he have at the beginning and will need to acquire as they proceed into the story. Show

how they will acquire those needed changes through your character's interactions with others. Show the influences which create the needed changes.

Example: In the *Karate Kid,* Daniel starts out as a mild, passive youngster and is attacked by bullies using karate. Daniel decides to take karate lessons. Mr. Miogi becomes his teacher and Daniel acquires his training through rather unconventional techniques, giving him the edge needed.

You may create your characters from the standpoint of where the story dictates the changes or others help your main character achieve their objective. If the story dictates the changes, try to use a personal connection such as background of the main character. Show how they affect the character in their current situation.

Show evidence of your character's philosophy within the story and express it through actions rather than dialogue. The audience should be able to see how she/he feels about other people and situations. In certain situations, dialogue is not necessary. For example, if a person has a serious problem against homosexuals, they show it. When they see an act of homosexuality being displayed, the person exhibits their displeasure through facial expressions such as a grimace or frown.

Net, the attitude of certain key characters should lead to specific actions. If the main character needs to be more sympathetic than usual, then check their emotional responses and the ways you **show** their emotional makeup. Attempt to broaden their emotional makeup, so you can stretch the character's ranges of self expression. Find a way to expand your character's emotions beyond the usual mad, scared, sad and glad. Try and **go for the**

gusto. Try rage, frustration, irritation or ecstasy. If your character is scared stiff or frozen with fear, then show them in action and show their true colors with an adrenaline rush as a result of the dangerous situation.

Reviewing and answering all of the questions listed below will help reveal and expand the realism of your character, while still advancing and keeping the story in focus.

As you examine your characters, ask yourself:

1. Have I become stuck in stereotyping characters?

2. Have I allowed my characters to be defined and grow through the three dimensions.?

3. Have I allowed my characters enough time to change and are their changes credible?

4. What are the influences upon my main characters that help them change?

5. Is there a catalyst character or does the story force the changes in my character?

6. Can I see clearly how the influences of the story and other characters create the transformation of the main characters through their images and actions?

Having answered these questions and applied your answers you will also enhance identity and the commercial viability of your material.

CHARACTER FUNCTIONS

Every character in your story must have an essential role to play. On occasion there are numerous stories that seem murky, muddy and bogged down. It could be a story problem because it's confusing, inconsistent and unstructured. But often it's a character problem. There could be too many characters and nothing for them to do. So, what are they doing there? Do they have a real purpose in the story?

Generally, in a two-three hour story, there's only a certain number of characters an audience can grasp at one time. When there are too many characters, they overwhelm viewers and make it more difficult to grasp the story. In most cases, there are five, six or seven at most, characters that will have a direct impact on the story itself. They might include such characters as: the antagonist, protagonist, a possible love interest and a couple of supporting characters.

So, ask yourself: Where or whom do I cut? You will have your favorite characters that are unique and memorable. But, unfortunately, favorites are not always workable.

Most new writers find it most difficult to cut characters. In order to cut efficiently, it is essential to begin looking at the character functions.

Let's divide the character functions into five categories: *Main, Supporting, Catalyst, Dimensional Characters and Thematic Characters.*

Main Characters

The main character is the person who is responsible for moving the story forward. They are the main focus of the story and provide the main conflict. They should be able to keep the story interesting for the duration.

The main character is the *protagonist*. She/he is who the story is about, the person who is followed, cheered, empathized with and/or esteemed. They are usually a positive figure, the hero or heroine of the story. That doesn't mean the person is perfect and without a flaw.

The audience may get angry about certain traits that are distasteful, but the protagonist commands the attention.

On occasion, the main character can be a negative character. The important part is that they get the audience involved and the audience see the story from this character's point of view. This character is the *antagonist*.

Sometimes the antagonist is a combination of people, such as a group of supporting characters whose main function is to prevent the protagonist from achieving his/her goal.

Supporting Characters

Supporting characters help and support the main characters in accomplishing their goals. Main characters need supporting characters to stand with or against them, or give information. They should be able to listen, advise, push or pull and somehow force the main character to make a decision.

Another function of a supporting character is to act as confidante or assistant. Unfortunately most of the time, the confidante is often a much less interesting person. They are usually shown as the person who the hero/ine confides in, rather than reveal themselves. Also, supporting characters are often used as an excuse for giving information, which causes the scene to get bogged down and filled with long expository speeches. Lengthy dialogue substitutes for good drama or action.

When developing **your** characters, think of the confidante as the person to whom the protagonist reveals themselves to, rather than tells. Don't make them a dull person. This should be a trustworthy person, in whose presence the protagonist can be him/herself.

Instead of always talking and listening, give the confidante an opportunity to make the hero/ine cry, laugh or be vulnerable, thus revealing other dimensions of the main character.

THE SET-UP

The most important pages of your story are in the first several pages. These are known as the *set-up*. The set-up gives all the vital information necessary to establish the main characters, the style, the theme of the story and the location. It defines the *genre*, i.e., drama, comedy, action, romance, tragedy or farce.

The set-up gives the reader, producer or director an idea of the spine and/or direction of the story and focuses the situation into a coherent storyline.

Some within the writer's community still believe that only television is written in what is commonly referred to as the three act format. Well, that would depend, to whom you were speaking as to whether or not that is true. A three act format consists of a beginning, middle and ending. Whether for television or feature film, both must have all three of these essential elements or **no** story can or will exist.

Three Act Format—Act One

Act one must contain four essential elements— *protagonist, antagonist,* the *plot/subplot* and the *or else factor*

1. The protagonist, the main character(s) a k a hero, heroine, the star.

2. The antagonist, bad guy, a k a villain, heavy. Never minimize or belittle this guy because your villain is all-important in several respects.

    His job is to drive the story to catastrophe. As you create this character, you can explore all the evil and awful pits within your imagination and then denounce them with touching piety, i.e., a religious belief or devotion to parents/family.

3. You need to **shake-up** your audience with a disturbance, disaster, problem or crisis. So as much as possible, open your story or script in crisis or something along that line. As in most dramas, suspenses or thrillers, subplots put the person(s) under a microscope. We will discuss *plots/ subplots* later in section two.

4. The *or else factor* or, as I like to refer to it as, The OH BOY!, factor means **what will be the fate in store for your hero/ine if they do not solve the problem and in time.**

    Example: In *Carlito's Way,* if Carlito, hadn't been able to distance himself from his past life in the mob, he would have been returned to prison or killed by the son of the man his attorney murdered.

    This factor is essential to charging the story with apprehension, expectancy or suspense.

TIP

Keep this one important factor in mind at all times as you write your story: EVERY written page of character and/or stage direction and dialogue represents one minute of film footage on the screen.

Act Two

Act two, the middle, includes the *turning point* in the plot or subplot of your story. This changes the direction of the story and forces the main character to action and results in the or else factor.

Act Three

Act three, the end, the *climax* of the story is where all the loose ends are connected.

Metaphor

A Metaphor tells us about the theme of the story through the pictures you create with your **words**. Your words are extremely important. You must be able to tell as much as you can within the first several pages or minutes. You must be able to get the reader in the mood of the story by creating a metaphor.

Example: If I were to say DOG, you didn't think of the word D-O-G. No, your imagination created a picture of an actual dog, some kind with which you may be familiar.

As you write, you **must** use words which paint a picture of what you want to convey to your reader.

Example:

We PICK UP and FOLLOW a St. Bernard dog as he CLIMBS UP the staircase.

We SEE him HIT a door with his PAWS and we HEAR a LOUD CRASH as the door comes OFF it's hinges.

As you can see in this example, you should be able to picture in your mind the action taking place, and also imagine the sounds you would hear as well. After the initial image, (something like an explosion, a murder, a letter arrives, or a phone call is received) the story should be developed.

SECTION ONE SUMMARY

The outline is the most important part in beginning your story. It gives you the basic information about your story and lays the foundation upon which to build and further develop your story.

After the outline, you need to create and/or develop all the characters in your story. In the outline you may have several main characters, but others will be necessary to complete the entire story. Make sure that the main characters, as well as supporting characters, are as unforgettable as possible.

In your character functions, make sure not to over do it, or have too many characters doing too many different and unimportant things. This confuses the story and makes it very difficult to follow.

The best place to develop your characters is in your *pyramid*, (see page 48). Not only can you use the pyramid to develop your story, but also to develop each character, their respective functions and how they will impact the story. Then, is when you should begin to set up your story.

Notes:

Section Two

Story Cohesiveness

Keeping Your Story Moving

Plots and Subplots

Turning Points

Catalysts

Making a Cohesive Script

Commercialization

Summary

The Pyramid

Story Cohesiveness

In this section, we will discuss various elements of screenwriting to bring more meaning and understanding to the topics discussed in Section One.

Section Two

KEEPING YOUR STORY MOVING

One of the hardest things for the majority of new writers is the challenge they face in building their story and keeping the story moving for 75-120 pages.

Most problems come from insufficient momentum and a lack of focus. If the story doesn't move and you're unsure as to what's happening and why, your story has moved from the spine.

Unrelated scenes slow down your story, and characters who are too talky or not acting will also slow down your story. It could be that you are missing and/or skipping beats. Or the story could be developing much too fast or too slow. To keep your story moving, create a strong *turning point*.

Momentum

Momentum occurs when one scene leads into the next. When scenes are connected in a cause-effect relationship, every scene advances the action, bringing it closer to the final climax. Although it may seem very complex, there is an easier way to make it work, as shown in the example below. In this murder mystery, we'll integrate the complexities and try to demonstrate the cause-effect relationship. For now, think of momentum as coming from action-reaction scenes.

Example:

Robert points out Harris as the murderer. This leads directly to the next scene. Harry visits Mark and tells him about Harris. Mark tells him to keep quiet about it.

This leads to the next scene:

Harry returns to his apartment, only to be shot at by Harris. He realizes Mark is also one of the murderers.

This leads to the next scene:

Harry picks up Joanne and James, borrows Sandy's car and drives them to the hometown bar.

This leads to the next scene:

As a result of his injury, Harry passes out.

This leads into the second act, with Harry hiding out at the bar, in the back room.

Notice how every scene is related to the next scene. This is called momentum. It continually pushes the story forward. There are some scenes that have only small story points. They may focus on the subplot or on a character's discovery.

If every scene would take us forward in a straight path, always advancing toward the climax, the story would lack subtlety and dimension.

Action Points

An action point is a dramatic event that causes a reaction. Usually, this reaction is caused by another action, which also depends on the genre.

Most action points are events and visualizations, as opposed to dialogue. An action point can appear in any scene. They are very important in the second turning point or scene, where the most momentum is needed for the longest period of time. The action points that are used most often are the *barrier*, the *complication* and the *reversal*.

The Barrier

A character tries to follow a clue or performs some type of action and it doesn't work. This leads to a dead-end. The character has hit a *brick wall* and must change directions and try something else or another action or direction. When this happens, they have just hit a *barrier*.

The barrier is an action point because it forces the character to make a new decision and take a new action or direction. Barriers stop the action for a brief moment.

However, the story doesn't develop out of a barrier. It develops out of a decision to try another action.

Example:

A door to door salesman goes to door #1 to sell his product. The customer says no. This is the first barrier. He goes to the next door. The customer still says no— the second barrier. He goes to the third door and finally, the third says yes! A sale is made. As a result, the salesman decides to take the rest of the day off to celebrate with his boss. The boss decides to give him a promotion; he gets a new office and no more door-to-door selling.

Here we see the barrier led to the other actions. But the real development and momentum came as a result of the last action when the barrier was overcome with the sale.

Barriers are used most often in detective stories, mysteries and action adventures.

TIP

Don't use too many barriers. It causes the story to become monotonous and stagnant. When used sparingly, barriers can push the story forward.

The Complication

Whereas a barrier pushes the story forward by forcing new directions and/or decisions, complications push forward by leading to an anticipated payoff. They create such momentum, you rarely need more than a couple in your story. The complication can be described when something happens, but the reaction doesn't come until later. The complication is not an ordinary plain action point. We have to wait in anticipation for the inevitable response. It's an action point that doesn't *pay off* immediately. It's quite rare and sometimes subtle.

To find a complication, check for these four essential elements:

a. Complications don't payoff immediately. They add anticipation to the story.

b. It's the beginning of a new subplot.

c. It doesn't turn the story around, it keeps the story moving forward.

d. It often gets in the way of a character and interferes with the overall intentions.

An excellent example of a complication is in the film *Tootsie*. Here we see a man, dressed as a woman, with intentions of landing an acting job.

1st complication. He sees a woman on the first day and falls in love with her, which could jeopardize his job.

2nd complication. An actor on the same soap falls in love with Tootsie.

3rd complication. The father of Tootsie's love interest falls in love with Tootsie also.

All of this puts Tootsie's career in total jeopardy.

The Reversal

A reversal is the strongest type of action point. It changes the direction of the story 180 degrees—positive to a negative or the other way around. It can work physically and/or emotionally. Reversals can reverse action or a character's emotional response. At the first or second turning point, a reversal can work very well in building momentum into the next scene. A reversal can often be created by strengthening an action point. You can create a strong emotional reversal by looking for emotional moments that can be expanded. If your main character is kind of sad, see if you can create despair, then "sorta" happy, leading to ecstasy for greater punch.

For example, in a detective story, a cop is discouraged because all the clues have ended with no results. Suddenly he puts two and two together to figure out how to solve the case.

Reversals catapult the story by forcing it into a new direction with new developments. One or two have sufficient power to push the story through the difficult second and/or third scenes.

Scene Sequences

Occasionally, action-reaction scenes are grouped together around one central mini story-line. Momentum is gained through action-reaction scenes, where each lead to the next, advancing the story forward toward the climax. For subplots, this is done without any interruptions. These type scenes are called, *scene sequences*. They are relatively short, ranging from three to six minutes in length.

Like action points, scene sequences can come at any place in the story. More often than not, most momentum problems occur because of an unclear scene or story structure without turning points to keep the story moving.

Some scenes may take the story on a tangent, rather than focus on the story line. A lot of momentum problems are misdiagnosed resulting in continuous unresolved problems. These problems are mostly seen in action adventures. Most filmmakers try to solve the problem by adding more action than necessary. When you see an additional car chase, fist fight or shoot-out, the story slows down.

Some filmmakers confuse momentum with pacing. They try to solve the problem by picking up the pace of the story. It may look as if the problem is a lack of momentum, if the story is **too** predictable and has no subplots to give dimension to the story.

TIP

Try watching several films, with the intent of identifying these elements. If the character is stereotyped, interest will diminish. Focus on the development of the plotline and, subplot, and themes will pick-up interest.

All of the aforementioned needs to be an integral part of your story. In order to use these elements, it's important to understand them. Many films will rely on one or more rather than a combination of all. Once you are clear on how these are used in other films, it will be much easier to find and develop them within your story. To create a scene sequence, you must find the scene that relates to the main idea. Begin stringing them together to create a setup, development and climax to the sequence.

Here are a few questions to ask yourself about action points in your story:

a. How are my action points used? Is my story gaining momentum through action or does it use dialogue to push the story forward?

b. What kind of action points are within my story? Where do they occur and how often do they occur?

c. Are there any scene sequences in my story? If so, where do they occur and how are they working to give energy to the story?

d. Does my story go off on tangents or does it stay focused on the plot and subplot lines?

e. Can I construct action points or scene sequences from dramatic elements already being used?

You do not need **big** action to move your story. Not every physical action needs a dramatic physical response. At times it can move with either physical, dialogue or emotional responses. As long as there are connections between one action and another and as long as there's the necessary structure for support, your story will stay on track. If you keep this concept in mind, you need not be concerned if your story is relational, slow-paced or fast-paced.

Action slows down for a love scene. As long as there are action-reaction scenes, the script will have direction, focus and momentum.

Don't impose something in your story if it's not important, but don't be afraid to be strong and dramatic. The story, particularly the second scene will need energy and punch to keep it exciting and keep the momentum flowing.

PLOTS AND SUBPLOTS

For decades many writers have debated whether or not, there is such a thing as an *original idea*, or only old ideas with new twists. What makes an old idea different? Subplots. The overall function of subplots is to give dimension to the story. Subplots deepen the story and carry the theme so it is not a straight linear action-oriented script. They reveal an extra dimension to the characters, such as: individual themes of identity, integrity, love, greed or finding one's self.

Subplots can also reveal a character's vulnerability. Often during the plot, the character is too busy to tell us about themselves, so in the subplot, we can see their goals, dreams and desires.

Subplots provide an opportunity for the main character(s) to relax, kick-back and do other things. They can also show the character's transformation of why and how.

Plotlines have a beginning, middle and end, which are the key events that happen to the character(s) in the story. Good subplots have turning points, clear set-ups, development and a payoff at the end. Turning points of subplots often reinforce the plotline by happening just before or right after the turning point of the plot.

If your subplot lines are carefully worked out, they can work anywhere. On the other hand, if there are too many subplots that are not well integrated, or if too much is going on, your story will become muddy, murky, unfocused and weighted. Too many can also cause a lack of structure and disorient the story to the point that no one knows what's going on.

TIP

Above all, remember that as long as there are actions and responses that are related to your story, your script will continuously move. Always analyze what kind of action points you use and how you keep the story moving.

While working your story, try to separate your plot from the subplot in order to distinguish between their differences. If you're unsure or they are too close in similarities to make a clear distinction between the two, get a note pad and answer these questions for yourself:

a. What is the real motivation or central problem?

b. Where does most of the action originate? More times than not, this is your plotline.

c. What message am I trying to convey? This is your subplot.

d. What's the theme of the story?

By separating your plot from subplot lines, you should be able to see how you have structured each and how they should work together. Look for the set-up in each. If you are still having difficulties distinguishing between the two, try to trace the plotline and subplot back to where they first begin. This is probably your first turning point. Follow its development to see where it takes another turn. Then ask yourself these questions:

a. Is this where my story becomes more urgent and intense?

b. Do I need this subplot and does it add to my story?

c. Does it intersect the story and/or give needed dimension to my story?

d. How many subplots do I have? If there are more than three, are they necessary?

e. Are there any subplots I can cut to give more focus to the plotline of the story?

f. Do I have a clear structure for each subplot, with clear set-ups, turning points and a clear climax in the story?

g. Does my subplot resolution occur close to the climax of the plotline?

If your subplot is tightly structured, dimensional in the story and intersects the plot, you will have a workable subplot.

Make sure that once the climax of the plot has happened, the climax of the subplot(s) has happened just as quickly.

TIP

Making sure your subplot(s) work is one of the most important jobs in writing your script/story.

TURNING POINTS

Turning Points are the unpredictable, intriguing twists and turns in your story which keeps it interesting along the way to its climax. To get a better understanding of turning points, compare writing to music.

The beats in music, put together, create a measure and then a phrase and then a melody and finally an entire song. Writing is the same. A single *beat* (twist or turn) placed together with another twist or turn create an entire scene.

The beats are not the main focus of the story, but they do prepare for what is to come next, *turning points*.

These twists and turns can happen throughout your story. But there are **two** turning points that need to happen at certain places to keep the story moving.

The first turning point should happen between pages 25 and 40 and then at 75 to 90. As a result of these turning points, new events occur and decisions are made. These turning points help the story achieve momentum and retain its focus.

Turning points accomplish a variety of functions:

1. They turn the action in a new and different direction.

   Example: A murder mystery. A young detective believes he's found the murder weapon (a knife), but later learns from the coroner that the holes in the body are too small, to be made by a knife, plus there are also bullet holes.

2. They raise the central question again and make us wonder about the answer or solution.

   Example: So, which of the two items is the actual murder weapon?

3. It's often a moment of decision or commitment making on the part of the main character.

   Example: The detective decides to follow his hunches on the knife being the weapon.

4. It often raises the stakes (if there are any).

   Example: The victim murdered just happened to be wealthy and had numerous individuals with motives for murder.

5. It pushes the story into the next scene or act.

   Example: He begins to try and focus on the individuals with the most to gain by the death of the wealthy victim.

6. It takes us into a new arena and gives a sense of a different focus of the action.

   Example: Political and departmental pressures give additional problems to the detective which further hampers his effectiveness.

As you can see, there are numerous twists and turns that can be derived from this brief set of circumstances.

Keep the events within your story as interesting as possible without giving away the answers. Although, a single turning point can and will accomplish all these functions, many turning points keep it more interesting.

Turning points give a sense of urgency and momentum to the story and push us forward, toward its conclusion.

Climax

The conclusion or *climax* usually happens one to seven pages from the end of the script, followed by a short resolution that ties up all the loose ends. The climax is the **END**. It's the moment when all the problems are resolved, the questions are answered, the tension eases and everything's okay. Once the climax is reached, the party is over and it's time to go home. There is nothing more to be said and it's a good idea, not to say anything else.

CATALYSTS

The initial image is called the *catalyst*. It's the main thrust that gets the plot moving. Someone has to make a decision, thus setting the main character(s) into motion.

Example: You get a phone call from a friend, informing you of a possible problem created by your previous actions and now you must make a decision as to what actions you will take to resolve the problem. The phone call you received is the catalyst.

There are three kinds of catalysts, *Action, Dialogue* and *Situation*.

Action: A murder has occurred and only one detective has the ability and skills to solve the case, i.e., *Columbo*.

Dialogue: A piece of information received by letter or a phone call, a note is found or a conversation between two characters takes place that sets the story in motion.

Situation: A series of incidents that add up over a period of time and builds until the spine of the story is revealed. The image may have oriented us and the catalyst has begun the story; but, the most important ingredient is still needed.

That ingredient is that *every story is a mystery* in some way and should ask a specific question in the set-up. Those questions *must* be answered in the climax a k a THE END.

Example:

A situation or problem (a murder) is introduced in the set-up (action). It *must* be resolved in the climax. Who did it and why!

Once the question is raised, everything in the story must relate to that question in some form. After the question is asked, the set-up is complete and now the story is ready to unfold.

As the story unfolds, tell more about main characters and depict them in action before you develop them in the next situation.

For instance:

Who or what is motivating the character(s)?

What's the central conflict?

What or who is making him/her do what they are doing or act the way they are acting?

Catalyst Characters

As previously shown, not only can an event be the catalyst, but another character can be a catalyst. This is the person who provides a piece of information or causes an event to happen that pushes the protagonist into action. Sometimes, the catalyst delivers a clue to help solve a mystery, or force the transformation of the protagonist. Almost every story has a catalyst.

The hero/heroine cannot do it alone. They need help in getting and keeping the story moving. When creating this character, it's important to make them as active as possible. They should catapult the story forward through action and not dialogue.

There are also smaller supporting roles whose main function is to demonstrate the prestige, power or stature of the hero/heroine or villain. They provide mass and weight to the story.

These characters are known as the body guards, secretaries, assistants, right-hand-men or girl Fridays which surround the powerful men and women. We are able to understand who's important, by the weight and mass necessary to communicate power.

If you need more mass, just add character functions to those characters. For instance, make the bodyguard, the confidante also. This gives the character more depth.

Dimensional Characters

There are those characters that always provide dimension to the story and to the main characters. This doesn't mean the character is dimensional, but the story becomes more dimensional because of that person.

There are serious films that have one funny person who provides the comic relief, or humor to lighten up the story and ease tension.

A couple of good examples are: Professor Brown in *Back to the Future* and Danny Devito in *Romancing the Stone* or the many characters of Arsenio Hall in *Coming to America*. These characters make us laugh and the humor is often focused on those characters.

By contrasting these characters, we can see the main character clearer, due to their differences. They expand the depth of the story and add texture, focus and clarity to subtle character traits.

TIP

Please be careful not to add too many people or you'll have clutter rather than mass. Too few will diminish power.

THEMATIC CHARACTERS

Characters who convey or express the theme of the story are called *thematic characters*. One or two of these characters are usually found in any film, whether action, romance, mystery or drama.

An example of a film with *theme oriented* characters can be found in films such as *The Color Purple*. The driving force behind your story should not be just the fascination with the story or characters, but the idea itself.

In thematically oriented stories, one character is the *balance character*. This character makes sure the theme is not misinterpreted. A good example is *A Passage to India*. This was a story about the problems, manipulations, exploitation and fascination between English and Indian relationships.

The Color Purple was criticized for its one dimensional portrayal of Black males because it seemed to give an unbalanced picture of Black men as a whole. The balance in this film could have been maintained by showing one character who represented just the opposite in Black men. Regardless of race, whether black on black, white on white or any combination, a positive must always be used to create the needed balance.

Thematic characters tend to add dimension to the theme of the story by showing differing points of view. This helps to communicate the idea.

Another character used to communicate the theme of the story is from the writer's *point of view* character. This character is often called the alter ego. If there's a particular philosophy or attitude the writer wants to convey, it can be given through either of these characters.

It's not always necessary for the audience to know the writers *point of view*. However, if you have a specific idea you want to get across in your story, choose a specific character who can do this for you. Never use the main character. Choose a supporting character with whom you can identify. This character becomes more essential to the story that's being told because the story is now dependent on the clear message the writer is conveying.

If you are working on a controversial topic where there's no clear cut right or wrong, help the audience think through the message to gain insight into the story.

Sometimes your story needs a character with whom your audience can easily identify. We call this an *audience point of view*. This is not always the protagonist, for whom we might feel empathy or sympathy. This character brings the reader and/or audience into the story by letting them know how they are to feel or think on a certain situation.

This point of view becomes even more important when the story deals with topics such as: the supernatural, psychics, reincarnation, etc. Most people tend to be skeptics regarding these topics. To make your story work on such topics and be more believable, choose a character who is also a skeptic and can represent the general skepticism of your audience. As the character changes and becomes more convincing along the way, the audience will also be carried along by the situation and change some of their attitudes. They can identify with the character and become involved even more so as the story unfolds. It doesn't mean that the story has made them believers, but it suspends their disbeliefs for a moment.

In some cases, characters fulfill more than one function. Regardless of the number of functions, it's important that these functions have a place and contribute to the story.

Clarifying your character's functions keeps the story focused.

Understanding Character Functions

In Section One, we discussed character functions and divided these functions into five categories. The following is designed to help you **further** understand character functions.

The script needs many characters. The reader wants to know what characters are important and what these key characters bring to your story. Keep the story focused while creating a background of characters to give the story texture. The audience wants to learn as much as possible in the first fifteen minutes of the story. Also during this time introduce the main characters. Your audience wants to know their names and be able to quickly identify them at a glance plus have a sense of what each is contributing to the story. During the writing, but mostly rewriting, it's essential to establish the story focus and clarify the character functions.

Once your story is purchased and goes into production, it becomes a casting problem. One of the best ways to make a specific character memorable is through ethnic type, weight, height or voice.

Often it may become necessary to cut a favorite character's function and/or combine it with another character more suitable in order to clarify character functions. It will be impossible for you to stay focused on the story if you keep trying to make changes midstream.

Wait until you complete the first draft before you begin to look at the characters in your story and clarify their major functions.

As you go through your story, ask yourself these questions:

1. Is my protagonist/main character driving the action?

    Does she/he achieve the climax of the story?

2. Do I have a confidante? If so, are they too talky?

    Can I have them show through actions as well as talk?

3. Am I missing a function?

    Do I need another catalyst so there will be no trouble in understanding the theme?

4. Is my protagonist receiving help from supporting characters?

TIP

Films where minorities play important roles need to be balanced by other positive roles as well. Without this balance, your story can be open to misunderstanding, criticisms, or worse, to protest, anger and perhaps not be purchased.

5. Do I have a character that carries my personal point of view?

   If so, have I kept that character active and dramatic as opposed to talky?

6. Does my point of view give insight into the story or just push a message?
   Or, am I trying to get my point of view across, so I just put it in there?

7. Am I dealing with a subject which is open to misinterpretation?

   If so, have I given both sides to the issue.

8. Have I created another character to show the reverse side of the story?

9. Do I have a clear cut picture of my protagonist and antagonist?

10. Do I know what the central issue or problem is?

11. Do I have comic relief (humor) in my story to ease tension or lighten up the material. If so, does only one character carry that comic relief?

12. Who are my supporting characters? Do they contribute to the story?

13. Do the catalyst characters in my story help move the story with action?

14. Does every character have a function in the story?

There have been many films which have failed because there were too many characters without a clear story function.

MAKING A COHESIVE SCRIPT

Most new writers loose touch with their storylines in their inability to create cohesiveness in their scripts. This is due to a lack of understanding of a few widely used concepts.

Films need to have a sense of unity and integration. This can come form the use of what is known as: *foreshadowing*, *motifs*, *repetition*, *contrasts* and *payoffs*.

Foreshadowing

Foreshadowing is a visual clue or piece of information that is paid off later in your story. An example of foreshadowing is when you see the camera zooming in on a knife or gun on the table in a murder mystery, and is later used in the commission of a murder. That's obvious foreshadowing and payoff.

Most films use some form of foreshadowing and payoffs. There are several types used. In comedies, it's a joke that sets-up the next response. Informative foreshadowing sets up what will happen.

The best form of foreshadowing is when an object or piece of information is set-up in one context and is considered subtle and unimportant, but later it becomes relevant with a surprising and unpredictable ending.

Just as an object can be used, dialogue can be used to plant some form of information that can seem irrelevant in one respect but highly important in another.

TIP

Character functions must take focus and perform clear, clean and easy to follow functions.

Motifs

These are images, rhythms and/or sounds that **repeat** and deepen, and add texture to the theme as well as give dimension to the storyline. They need to be repeated at least three or four times to work well. They work best when used continually throughout the entire film, helping to keep the focus on certain elements.

The best example of a recurring motif is in the film *JAWS*. Whenever the shark came near and was about to strike, you would hear a DUM-DUM-DUM-DUM-DUM sound, except for the initial attack of the shark.

A visual motif is seen in *Ghostbusters,* where we see the lion at the library first, then in Dana's refrigerator as a possessed dog.

Repetition

This is anything that repeats itself, such as an idea, image or sound. Even sounds in dialogue, character traits, or the use of a combination of all can be used to stay focused on the main idea.

Example:

If you were doing a story on a drug addict, you might start by repeating certain information. First, showing them making a drug buy, then in a secluded place either smoking it or shooting-up; then, showing the effects of the usage through hallucinations; then going through the house, room to room, in a frantic search for funds to make another buy; finally, showing them being found in an alley, dead or overdosed as a result of their actions.

By using a variety of images and characteristics in your story, you will be able to keep focused by threading this information throughout the script.

Contrast

Just as repetition helps keep the script focused, so does the use of *contrast*. Contrast allows you to show opposites and help make the connections by showing differences between characters. Opposites do attract and by contrasting two characters, the strongest character dynamics are achieved. *Lethal Weapon*, *48 HRS.* and others that are relational stories, whether a romance, a partnership, or a friendship, will contain contrasting characters.

Contrast can reflect behavior and attitudes. Ethnic background, economic class and methods of approaching problems are ways to show contrast. Sometimes the contrast is psychological.

In the TV series, *Moonlighting*, the contrast between Maddie and David can be described in terms of inner fears, as well as outer characteristics. Maddie is a bubble detached from her emotions and David's emotions are very raw and on the surface. The thing they're most afraid of is falling in love with someone, (each other) and being exposed. Maddie protects herself with facial expressions and a cold exterior and David with his fast talking jive. Immediately, you have two characters who happen to have an enormous bond going on underneath and we see the push-pull in their relationship.

In *Fatal Attraction*, Beth and Alex are contrasting characters: one lighthearted, one depressed; one a caring wife, one a manipulative mistress; one involved with family, one single; one optimistic about her life, one desperate and pessimistic about the direction her life is taking.

You can use a contrast in character differences, scenes, locations, texture and energy.

For example, a peaceful sunset on a quiet beachfront, then a dark, noisy and smoke-filled bar.

PAYOFFS

Payoffs are the result of or the climax to foreshadowing. As previously mentioned, if you use an object or piece of information in the beginning to start the action, you **must** use it in the ending in some way to ensure closing all the loose ends.

For instance, a murder mystery—if you use a gun, knife or club in the beginning and it's used in killing someone, it must show up again as the detective somehow finds the gun and ties it to the killer. When you begin the rewriting process, make sure that everything you have foreshadowed is paid off.

After several rewrites, you may discover that some foreshadowing might have been dropped or may need to be dropped from one rewrite to the next.

TIP

Be careful to follow every thread of your story as not to leave loose ends.

Checklist

1. Is everything I have paid-off, foreshadowed in the story?

   Have I found original ways to foreshadow and/or payoff certain information?

2. Have I changed functions or disguised foreshadowing information?

   Have I used humor to set up and payoff other information?

3. Have I created or implied motifs that could be used to integrate the script visually?

4. Have I thought through my story visually, repeating images that will give a sense of cohesiveness?

5. Have I contrasted scenes, characters, action and images to give my story a more dramatic texture and punch?

6. Have I done at least one rewrite during which I tried to see the story as a whole, rather than focus on the individual parts?

The rewrite stages give you the opportunity to pull these relationships of your characters together. It's a chance to expand on themes and images by threading them throughout the story.

COMMERCIALIZATION

No matter how good or great a writer you are or think you might be, there is one important question that every producer will ask: Is it **COMMERCIAL**?

Everyone has different ideas and opinions concerning what makes a script commercial. Many producers think it's a matter of packaging, i.e., *get the right actors and/or directors.* Some say it's the subject matter, as they look for trends, i.e., what's in the news, (which is an excellent source). Some on the other hand think it's looking for an exciting new bestseller, i.e., a novel to make into a film.

In some cases, all of the above are true, but not even the most successful actors or directors, regardless of their names or past accomplishments, are able to take a poorly written script and carry it into a film and make it work. Trends come and go extremely fast, as quickly as the wind changes directions.

Not all bestsellers make good films and as usual there are those exceptions to the rule.

Now, before we go any further, you may ask, what about those *sequels*? Can't I write a sequel to an existing film? Well, yes and no! Depending on how deep your pockets are. Yes, if you can find out what studio owns the rights to the original version of the film of your intentions. And, if they are willing to sell their rights to you. At what price? **$$$$$$**. The prices often range anywhere from $100,000 up to $1,000,000.00 or higher. So the real answer is no! If you are not the original author, it's in your best interest not to waste your valuable time. For every theory about commercial success, be it a novel or sequel, there seems to be examples that disprove certain points.

But, there are certain elements that contribute decisively to the success or failure of a film. And, it's not dependent on the writer's close relationship to the producer, director, actor, or studio executive.

Here are the four essential elements considered to be absolute necessities in making a script successful and salable to all of the aforementioned individuals.

(a) Proper format

(b) Script and/or story structure

(c) Originality and creativity

(d) Marketability

If any of these are missing from your script, there's a very good chance that your story/idea and/or script will not sell. If somehow it does, the odds of your work being purchased again in the future are extremely slim. The reason being, the producer will have to hire another writer to rewrite the script and include all the things which you left out, adding to his production budget.

Structure by itself means very little without creativity and originality. When a producer speaks of creativity, they always mean, **"Is it fresh"?** Is it an original idea? Is it different as well as unique? Does it have a hook? Is it compelling as well as entertaining? Am I grabbed by the premise, i.e., storyline and/or theme?

TIP

Don't just depend on the newspapers, radio or television as a source for your creations. Use life itself as a guide and point of reference also.

Most successful commercial films are based on an original idea/story or premise that is well executed. Without something special that is upheld by good writing, it will be difficult to make a good script sale. Proper format alone won't make it. Creativity alone won't make it. Marketability isn't limited to packaging the project with the right people or based on the whims of an executive. But, a combination of all the elements will greatly increase your chances for success, not only at the box office, but future sales as well.

Story structure is not always clear in the first draft due to a lack of understanding and development. Sometimes several themes conflict with others. That's the job of rewriting. It gives you an opportunity to make a pyramid of your story/ideas.

Think of your main idea as the base of the pyramid and begin layering all the ideas associated with your theme on top of it. As you begin to build your pyramid, (see example on page 48), other ideas will begin to emerge with some more interesting than others. You should be able to see clearer how to structure your story and say what you really want to say. As you continue to build your pyramid, various ways to execute new ideas will come to mind as your theme becomes clearer.

Ask yourself these questions:

1. Can I say my theme in one paragraph of ten lines or less?

2. Does it remind me or will it remind others of any other stories? If so, what story and what's the difference in mine?

3. Is my theme expressed through action rather than dialogue? Do the images help expand or extend my theme?

4. Have I stayed away from having characters giving messages? If not, are the messages necessary?

5. Have I been willing to give up a smaller theme if it conflicts with the main theme of my story?

6. Have I considered how the readers, producers, etc. might respond, given their different lifestyles and conditions?

7. Have I looked at my personal connection or beliefs? How do they play into my story? This is one of the most important areas you *must* look at as you write your story.

TIP

If your story isn't tight and doesn't make sense, it will not make a good sale.

SECTION TWO SUMMARY

Always remember that the catalyst can be a person or event needed to push or move your story and gets the plot and subplots moving forward. Plots are the base of your story. It's what the story is about. The subplots deepen and add dimension to not only the story, but characters also.

When using turning points they should add the element of unpredictability with intriguing twists and turns throughout your story. It will be easier to keep your story moving as long as there are actions and responses that are related. As long as there are connecting actions, the necessary structure to support your story will keep your story on track.

To insure that your story is cohesive, make sure that all the elements of foreshadowing, motifs, repetition, contrast and payoffs are used effectively and properly. If at anytime you are unsure, always refer back to the checklist at the end of the section or topic as a point of reference and guide.

Making your story commercial is your ultimate goal. Whether you use the newspaper, a TV news story, radio or real life as a point of reference, always make sure you have incorporated the four essential elements necessary to make your story/script successful.

THE PYRAMID:

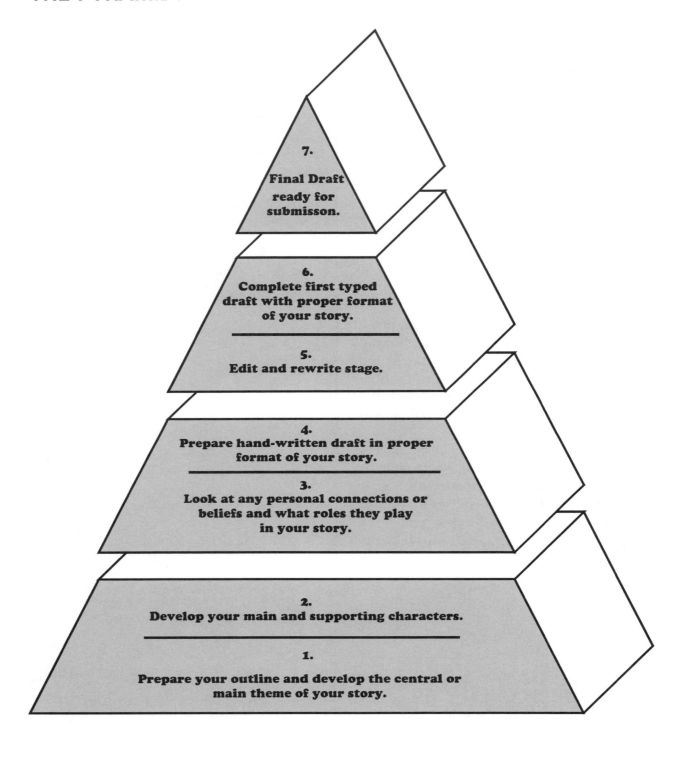

7.
Final Draft
ready for
submisson.

6.
Complete first typed
draft with proper format
of your story.

5.
Edit and rewrite stage.

4.
Prepare hand-written draft in proper
format of your story.

3.
Look at any personal connections or
beliefs and what roles they play
in your story.

2.
Develop your main and supporting characters.

1.
Prepare your outline and develop the central or
main theme of your story.

Notes:

Section Three

Screenplay Design & Layout

The Proper Format

Tab Settings

Personal Direction

Dialogue Rules

Stage Direction

Character Cues

Summary

Screenplay Design & Layout

Section Three gives you all the information on the proper way a screenplay must be presented. Following the layout shown will ensure accuracy of your well developed screenplay.

Section Three

PROPER FORMAT FOR FILM AND TELEVISION

When creating your script for feature film or television, use a typewriter, IBM compatible or Macintosh computer.

Use the following margins and tab settings for typewriter. The left edge of the paper must be at number (1). The following tabs **must** be at these settings for correctness.

19   Direction (stage and camera cues) ends at 72

29   Character dialogue and ends at 60

36   Character or personal direction, ends at 55

43   Character names

62   Scene endings

72   Page numbers, optional typed at 43 top page, centered.

IMPORTANT NOTE: The first letter of the character's name must start at (43) and move from left to right and above the dialogue. You will hear from a variety of others that you should also number the scenes as well in order to keep your pacing. I totally disagree. That will be the job of the director and his production staff.

Due to the numerous changes that will be made to your script if it is purchased, more times than not, the director will make the changes and put it into a shooting script format. Also, he will move scenes around to get a better feel for the piece. So, just forget it!

Example:

Heading followed by Direction: (See actual size in *Reference Section*.)

Direction can be multiple lines, more than two, but no more than six, depending on information described.

EXT. BEVERLY HILLS, LOS ANGELES - DAY - WIDE ANGLE MANSION

We SEE the SKYLINE of Beverly Hills and we PAN and WIDEN to SEE several MAN-SIONS with their well manicured lawns.

We ZOOM IN on ONE specific MANSION and we PICK UP and FOLLOW a person as they SCAMPER from the residence at a rather BRISK PACE.

TAB SETTINGS

For Screenplays:

19	Direction(s)
29	Dialogue
36	Personal direction
43	Character Name/cues
62	Scene endings
72	Page numbers (optional, can be placed at 43).

For Television:

11	Direction(s)
21	Dialogue
36	Personal direction
61	Character Name/cues
72	Scene endings

For Standard Live (soaps or sitcom):

11	Direction(s)
16	Dialogue
31	Personal direction
72	Character Name/cues

General Rules

1) Do not break a sentence from one page to another. The sentence must be completed before going on to the next page.

2) Always leave two spaces after punctuation at the end of a sentence.

3) When using the ellipsis (. . .) to indicate a pause within a sentence or an understood word or thought, leave a space after the last dot.

4) Use dashes and hyphens to indicate a pause in the same way as the ellipsis. Use dashes with a space on each side.

5) Always spell out the word "okay".

Condensing

Condensing is a method sometimes used to shorten the length of a screenplay thus enabling it to fit within a certain number of pages.

It is a practice frowned upon since it involves some distortion of the format which consequently violates the one (1) page = one (1) minute of screen time formula.

If condensing is requested of a typist by a writer, the following methods are possible ways of doing so. Take into consideration that if you do condense, you will have to deal with the situation at a later date.

1) Double-space (instead of triple space) between scenes.

2) Make full pages.

3) Do not use "(CONTINUEDS)" at the bottom or top pages. It is assumed that the scene will continue on until a CUT TO:, FADE TO:, etc. appears to end the scene.

4) Eliminate the use of continuing from dialogue interrupted by direction, unless it's absolutely necessary to use it.

PERSONAL DIRECTION

Personal direction should be used sparingly. It should consist of short instructions intended for a particular character only, such as: sits down, laughs evilly, stops, wipes brow, etc. Personal direction always appears directly under the character cue and in parenthesis, at tab (36) and ends at (55) with approximately (19) letters and spaces long, with all words in lower case—the only exception being nouns. The second line and all subsequent lines are indented one space, so the first letter falls directly below the first letter in the direction.

The direction may occur more than once in a given segment of dialogue, but the basic rules are the same throughout. If more than four lines long, it must be pulled out to the margin and shown above, i.e., *Robin looks up*.

Example:

                    JAMES
              (leans forward)

                    JAMES
              (holding the note moving to
              ward Michael)

                    JAMES
              (uncertain)
          I can't believe . . . I could be . . .
              (beat)
          It was Mr. Jones . . . yes I'm sure!

Long Passages

Incorrect:

>   JOHNSON
>   (thoughtfully puffing on his
>   Jamaican cigar, pacing back
>   and forth in front of the
>   window)

Correct:

>   Johnson, thoughtfully puffing on his
>   Jamaican Cigar, pacing back and forth
>   in front of the window.

Incorrect:

>   HOLMES
>   (to Watson in the next room)
>   I think I have it, Watson. Come take a
>   look at this.
>
>   (Watson enters)
>
>   The clay from his boots is red in color
>   like that found on the Sussex Moors.

Correct:

>   HOLMES
>   (to Watson in the next room)
>   I think I have it, Watson. . . . Come
>   take a look at this!
>
>   Watson ENTERS.
>
>   HOLMES
>   (continues)
>   The clay from his boots is red in color
>   like that found on the Sussex Moors.

Note: Never ever end a page with personal direction. When breaking dialogue from one page to the next, the break comes before the personal direction.

Personal direction should be placed on the next page, rather than left dangling at the bottom of the page. It should never end a passage of dialogue. If the direction is only one or two words, it's best to pull it out to the stage direction margin as shown on this page, i.e., Watson ENTERS:

RULES FOR DIALOGUE

Considering all words spoken are the characters' vehicles by which a film moves, it stands to reason that those spoken words are extremely important.

Dialogue is sacred. Dialogue begins at the center of the page and is relatively short, starting at tab (29) and ending at (62) in upper and lower case letters.

Spelling and Grammar Rules

First and foremost, if you do not have access to a word processor or computer with a built in dictionary with synonyms, go and find a dictionary. A dictionary is essential in your ability to spell various words correctly and it will amaze you how your vocabulary will begin to expand.

There are many rules which apply to standard grammar. But, there aren't specific rules when it comes to the wide variety of dialects used. It is advisable to get a dictionary of slangs which will assist you with character creation and dialogue.

Spell It Out

1. One and two digit numbers are always spelled out. Three or more digits may be written numerically.

2. Personal Titles, except for Mr., Mrs., etc., may be abbreviated.

3. Indications of time. (Five-fifteen).

4. There are numerous other words that might be tempting to abbreviate such as: Doctor and etc. But, when in doubt, spell-it-out.

No (-) Hyphenations

1. As a general rule words should not be hyphenated from one line to the next, with exceptions of words which are normally hyphenated. Words such as father-in-law and the like may be extended to the next line.

2. Pauses in a sentence may be indicated with the ellipsis and/or dashes and one space must be left before and after each usage.

3. The ellipsis is also used when a sentence is interrupted by personal direction. In such cases, it must appear at the end of the break and the beginning of the remainder of the sentence.

4. Paragraphing may be used where long passages of dialogue exist, but that practice is rare. Usually, paragraphing is used to indicate a change of thought.

Breaks in Dialogue

There are times when a character has lengthy dialogue that must be continued to the next page. Always remember to break the dialogue at the end of the sentence. The only exception is a stream of consciousness speech with no punctuation other than ellipsis or dashes, then the break should be made at the pause.

TIP

If you are asked to type a script for someone else, it is essential that you not change or alter the dialogue without consulting with the writer or those individuals accountable.

To indicate broken dialogue, the word *MORE* must be used, implying that the character speaking has more to say on the next page. MORE always appears capitalized and in parenthesis, single spaced down from the last sentence of dialogue and centered at tab (43).

Continued, Continues, Continuing

As a general rule of thumb, when you go from one page to the next, some would say to use the word *CONTINUED* or *CONTINUES* at the bottom of the page to show the scene hasn't ended. When CONTINUED or CONTINUES is used in dialogue, it must appear next to the character cue, in upper case in parenthesis and abbreviated. When dialogue moves from one page to the next without stage or personal direction, CONTINUES is used below to show more continued dialogue.

CONTINUING or CONTINUED should only appear when there are scene numbers used, which the producers staff will use after the script goes into development/preproduction. It is advised that you DO NOT use it.

Since it is assumed that if the terms FADE TO:, IN:, or OUT: , etc. doesn't appear, it will automatically be assumed that the scene will continue to the next page.

Example:

> MICHAEL
> Dialogue is continued . . . and so on

If during the dialogue, there's a break for character direction, then it should appear in lower case as shown:

> MICHAEL
> (continues)

The ellipsis used as a pause, with character direction interruptions:

> (MORE)
> (CONTINUES)

(starts new page)

> MICHAEL(CONTD)
> It's possible he could . . . be alive.

He SLOWLY walks closer to the body laying on the floor face down.

> MICHAEL
> (continues)
> But! . . . What if I'm wrong and he's dead?

Reaching the body, he hesitates in touching it, but his curiosity compels him forward.

> MICHAEL
> (continues)
> I was right the first time.
> (touches neck)
> He is alive!
> (touches wrist)
> But, . . . the pulse is weak!

NOTE: Use CONTINUES or CONTINUED or (CONTD) in character cue, dialogue, and after the break in dialogue with stage direction. For character dialogue to be continued on the next page, use (MORE), followed by a character cue, dialogue and personal direction within the dialogue and the use of ellipsis.

Keep in mind that there are times when character direction is interrupted by stage direction. When that happens the character cue must be restated after the direction with (continues) one space beneath at tab (36) and in parenthesis. Continues(ing) is always used to continue a character's dialogue, regardless of where that dialogue is interrupted by stage direction—even if it falls at the top, middle, or bottom of the page.

Relationship Between Continue and Beat

When *continuing* or *beat* are used along with personal direction, a semicolon (;) must be used to separate one from the other.

Example:

HORACE
(continuing; nervously)

or

HORACE
(beat; to Jerry)

or
(continuing; beat)

The only time when it's not necessary to use *(continuing)* is when a character's dialogue shifts from a *(V.O.)* situation to live dialogue. The infrequency in which this will happen is extremely rare, but when or if it does, think of *(V.O.)* and live dialogue as two different entities.

From (V.O.) To Live Dialogue

Jeremy STARES out the window and we HEAR his thoughts as he ponders the day's events.

JEREMY(V.O.)
I just know there has to be a connection between this brooch and my missing sibling. . .

Maybe they may have the other half or . . .

Jeremy WALKS over to the desk and PUSHES the speaker button and a number.

JEREMY
(continues)(a beat; to Ronald)
Hey Ron! . . . Pull your file on the Federated Acquisition and give me the location

STAGE DIRECTION

Stage direction refers to scene and character description, camera cues, sound cues and various other bits of information needed to facilitate the action, idea and storyline. It should include only the essential information necessary to create the desired effect.

Example:

Harry GETS UP from the desk and WALKS over to the window, STARES OUT for a brief moment, TURNS on his heels.

EXTREME CLOSE UP - HARRY'S EYES

The ANGER we SEE in Harry's eyes, words dare to describe. *(Word brevity and economy is essential).*

Stage direction begins at margin (19) and ends at tab (72). It is always double spaced down from the scene heading and extends across the page to the right margin in a single spaced format.

Composite Stage Direction

Example:

EXT. FOREST - DAY - (SPRING)

A purple haze is slowly MOVING over the lush forest. We HEAR a version of Tiny Tim's *Tiptoe Through the Tulips* in the f.g. as the CAMERA ADJUSTS, PANS to PICKUP and FOLLOW Robin as he walks down the path.

Suddenly, O.S. we HEAR the sound of twigs BREAKING in the b.g.

Robin LOOKS UP to SEE a rather LARGE monstrous size man STARING down upon him.

                    MAN
          If you dare move . . . it will be your
          very last ever. . . . . . .

Each of the examples shown above should be double spaced between each direction, except for the latter. It is first single spaced in a continuous flow of information, then double, then triple spaced between the direction and character cue.

TIP

Endless details and minute descriptions will only create useless clutter, which the reader or producer must wade through to get to the meat of your story. Such elaborate details are not necessary in your script.

Camera Cues At Work in Stage Direction

The following is an example of camera cues in stage direction.

Example:

WE ZOOM IN on a CLOSE-UP of the gun used in the murder.

We PICKUP and FOLLOW Joanne as she ENTERS from the foyer and MOVES to the kitchen and on into the study.

A moment later we SEE the police detective ENTER the room and we FOLLOW him over to the desk, where he PICKS UP the gun carefully.

We suddenly HEAR a door SLAM in the b.g. and the policeman PAUSES momentarily - - continues his investigation.

Capitalization

Capitalization of certain words is the means used to spotlight specific technical instructions, sound or camera cues and directions. It is also used when first introducing a character and their names. All characters with speaking roles must be capitalized each time they speak.

Abbreviations

Many words such as personal titles may be abbreviated in direction, but not in dialogue. There are four specific terms that require abbreviation in direction:

1)   f.g.   (foreground)

2)   b.g.   (background)

3)   O.S.   (OFF-SCREEN)

4)   M.O.S.   (Without sound)

Take note: O.S. is the correct term used in screenplays or television made for TV movies.

O.C. - OFF-CAMERA is used in taped formats for television, (sitcoms, variety shows, etc.).

CHARACTER CUES

The character cue is the name of the character to whom lines of dialogue are or will be assigned. Usually, the character is designated by either the first or last name but a role designation may be used instead.

Character cues are always stated in capital letters and start at tab (43), with the first letter of the name at (43), which is the center of the page. Personal titles are usually abbreviated in the cues. It is important to keep the character cues short and succinct, so that confusion is kept to a minimum.

Example: MR., MRS., SGT., CAPT., DR., etc.

While the camera might be on a character on the phone, we can hear the voice of the respondent on the other end, without ever seeing that other person. This is always a VOICE OVER situation.

Roles in Parenthesis

There are certain characters with specific roles, which must be designated in the character cue along with the name. This information should always appear capitalized, in parenthesis and next to the character's name.

Example:

GEORGE(PRIEST), MORRIS(DET.), etc.

There are some characters with only a role designation without a name, such as BARTENDER, BYSTANDER, NURSE or REPORTER. Then, you may use their role designation instead of a name.

There are times when you might have more than one character in the same role, but played by different characters. To distinguish which is speaking, use numbers, i.e., BARTENDER (#1) or (#2) etc.

Character Capitalization

When a character is first introduced in direction and has lines of dialogue, the name is always capitalized. After that, when s/he appears in direction, the name is in upper and lower case.

Understand however that capitalization is **not** necessary if the character is merely mentioned, but doesn't have a speaking role. Then the name is not capitalized. You can usually tell if a character will have a speaking role, by the amount of detail used in their introductory description.

Occasionally, a minor character may not have a speaking role but may be called upon for a significant emotional reaction. In this case and others, it may be appropriate to capitalize the introduction of that character.

Consistency

Consistency in the character cues throughout the script is essential. You may start out with their first name and then switch to the last throughout the remainder.

Whether the first name or last is used isn't important. But, whatever name you use, make sure it's consistent from the beginning to the end of your script.

Tab Settings For Feature Film

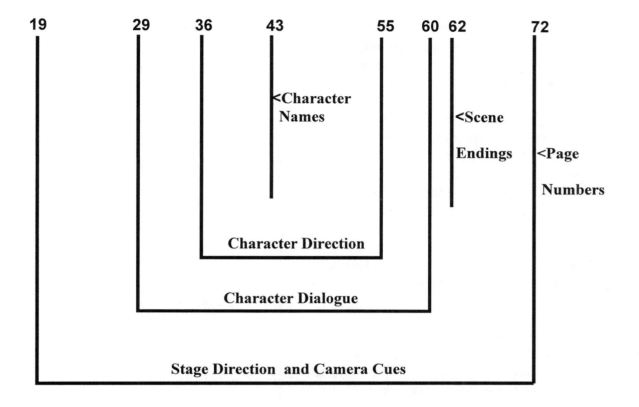

19   Begin Stage direction and camera cues; ends at 72.

Note Page #'s also 72 but at top of page in the right corner.

29   Character dialogue; ends at 60

36   Character and personal direction; ends at 55

43   Character Names

62   Scene Endings

72   Page numbers

SECTION THREE SUMMARY

When formatting your script, remember never use scene numbers in your submission version. With the numerous changes that will be made once purchased, the director and production staff will rearrange the scenes as deemed necessary.

As long as you use the correct tab setting, you will meet the required formatting rules. Personal direction should not be over used. If it extends beyond 19 letters, tab 55, two lines, then it must be pulled out to tab 19 as stage direction.

In stage direction, word brevity and economy is essential. Endless details tend to clutter the story.

Dialogue is sacred and must be treated as such. With the numerous languages, dialects and slangs used in our society and around the world, it stands to reason that, there are general rules regarding grammar. But remember, there are some rules which do not apply, depending upon the character.

Character cues are the identity of your character or his/her name and must be in all caps and consistent throughout the story.

Notes:

Section Four

Miscellaneous Topics

Paragraphing

Sound Cues

Scene Headings

Scene Endings

V.O. and O.S.

Summary

Miscellaneous Topics

Do not allow this heading to mislead you in anyway. Although the title may denote a degree of varied unimportance, the topics in this section are **extremely** important, and should be adopted as standards. Without them, your screenplay cannot and will not exist or work.

Section Four

PARAGRAPHING

Paragraphing in stage direction is fairly frequent. Whenever it is necessary, standard paragraphing should be used. Whereas in standard paragraphing, spaces are used to denote change in thought. In stage direction, it is separated by a period. It may not always be obvious to know where paragraphing should occur. The best way to determine where paragraphing should occur is by separating the description of a location from the information regarding the action in the scene. It can be used effectively to create force.

Example:

The sun has just began to set and there's a MIST HOVERING in the valley below. Hosea stands fixed and unmoving on the edge of the ledge of the mountain, overlooking the valley. There's no sign of his cohorts and the ransom money. He TURNS slowly and we SEE the anguish on his face. (See another example in Section Five).

Note: The first sentence gives the description of the location, i.e., sunset and a hovering mist in the valley below. From the second sentence on, the information regarding the action in the scene is described, separated only by a period.

Breaking Sentences

There are two techniques used to indicate a pause or break in a sentence—the Ellipsis (3 periods . . .) or (2 dashes --). When using the ellipsis at the end of a sentence, leave a space after the third period. When using two dashes, leave a space before and after the dashes. See example in sample script in Section Five.

Breaks in Direction

A passage of direction may be broken from one page to the next as long as the break comes at the end of a sentence. If the sentence is unusually long, the break could conceivably occur at an ellipsis or the dashes.

If the direction is broken, it is necessary to use CONTINUED, double spaced down at tab (62) and repeated on the next page at the top of the page at tab (19). This is one of those special occasions when CONTINUED should be used.

Whenever it is stated that a character enters or exits a scene, the words *ENTER* or *EXIT* need to be capitalized. Sometimes, the character will not speak immediately after the introduction, but will in a few lines a page or so later. It's always a good idea to scan ahead a couple of pages to see if the character indeed does have lines of dialogue that may have been overlooked during the initial rewrite.

SOUND CUES

Sound cues are those sounds which require some type of mechanical reproduction. It could be a train whistle, a knock on the door, a dog barking in the background, etc. Only the first word indicating the sound need to be capitalized, which gives the technician a key that his efforts are required. There's a tendency to capitalize all words constituting sound cues. Although it's not wrong, it is unnecessary.

It's important to be able to distinguish between actual sound cues requiring some kind of technical reproduction and those which would be made by the character(s) on the spot. Sounds made by character(s) are not considered sound cues and do not require capitalization.

At times certain sounds may need to be exaggerated, such as the sound of a punch or kick to another character. Obviously, there are sounds that cannot actually be made by the character. Those must be capitalized.

Example:

A) We HEAR a SMALL dog BARKING in the b.g. as the man approaches the front door of the house.

not a sound cue

B) Michelle THROWS a glass against the wall with a crash.

Consider the difference as with a dog. It would be somewhat difficult to get it to bark on cue at a specific moment without having a dog located nearby. It would require unnecessary location technical work.

SCENE HEADINGS

There are **two** basic scene headings, the masters, which are generally designated by INT. or EXT. (Interior and Exterior). There are shots that indicate more specific information that's found within the master scene, i.e., *angles, POV, and inserts, etc.* These are discussed later.

It is highly recommended that first time writers limit the use of shots and angles used in the script. It will make the reading a lot smoother and easier to digest and follow. Camera cues in direction such as: WIDEN TO REVEAL, FOLLOW, FIND, MOVE, WE SEE, and so on, can be used more effectively to eliminate the need for many shots and angles.

Scene and shot headings are **bits** of information used to designate various segments in which a film is broken down. As you prepare to write your story, think of your eyes as a **camera**. Whatever the camera sees is what the reader/audience will see. All scenes are and should be written from their POV (Point of View). It's your way of taking the reader through a sequence of events and directing their attention to those things that are important for them to notice.

On occasion, it's important for them to see something from a certain character's vantage point, i.e., to see what s/he is looking at through their eyes. This scene heading is called a Point of View (POV). Each heading is **highlighted**, by isolating it at the margin (19) and in all capital letters with each entity separated by a dash. Therefore, reading the basic information contained in each scene becomes easier to read at a quick glance. (See *"Using Scene Entries* *and Headings"*). The following are important format guidelines, which can be used as a guide to insure correct layout of your script.

Format Guidelines

A. Capitalize all entries in a scene heading.

B. Use triple spacing between each scene.

C. Never leave a heading standing alone at the bottom of the page.

D. Always accompany scene heading with at least one sentence of direction and/or dialogue. There's only one exception, that being an ESTABLISHING SHOT, and an occasional INSERT.

E. Scene headings always begin at margin (19) and end at tab (72).

F. When scene headings are particularly long, they must be extended to a second line and single spaced down.

G. These words MUST always be abbreviated.

   1. INT. and/or EXT. (Interior/Exterior)

   2. MED. SHOT or MED. CLOSEUP, etc.

   3. POV (Point of View)

   4. DR., SGT., CAPT., MR., MRS., and others that are similar are personal titles may also be abbreviated.

H. Do not underline scene headings.

I. To separate the two elements, use a slash (/) in the heading, never use dashes (- -).

Using Scene Entries and Headings

Below are specific elements of a scene heading arranged in their proper order.

1. INT. or EXT. Locations

2. TIME of DAY

3. CAMERA ANGLES and,

4. WHAT (The specific object or person the camera is on).

INT. or EXT. locations and the TIME of DAY are considered general broad categories. Then the categories narrow down to the CAMERA ANGLES and then more specific to WHAT the subject is.

Example: EXT. LOS ANGELES - DAY - WIDE ANGLE -MANSION

Exterior location - Time of day - Camera angle - Subject or Object.

When the subject, i.e., person or an object is the last entry in the heading, it is referred to in the first line of direction.

Example: Heading followed by Direction.

EXT. BEVERLY HILLS, LOS ANGELES - DAY - WIDE ANGLE - MANSION

We SEE the SKYLINE of Beverly Hills and we PAN and WIDEN to SEE several MAN-SIONS with their well manicured lawns.

We ZOOM IN on ONE specific MANSION and we PICK UP and FOLLOW a person as they SCAMPER from the residence at a rather BRISK PACE.

Scene Headings You Need to Know

(A) INT. RESTAURANT - NIGHT

This heading establishes the location as inside of the interior of an area and the time of day. Interior or Exterior should always appear first in the heading followed by the time of day.

(B) EXT. MANSION - DAY -CLOSE-UP - SHERREE

This heading establishes the where, the exterior on a location, the when or time of day, the camera angle and finally the object (who in this case) as a specific camera subject.

Picking up on Errors. If the camera angle and subject are placed in the opening direction by mistake, that information must be changed and placed correctly in the entries in the heading.

Incorrect:

EXT. MANSION - DAY

Close angle on Sherree as she's about to enter the Mansion.

Correct:

EXT. MANSION - DAY - CLOSE-UP - SHERREE

As she's about to ENTER the Mansion.

TIP

It is easy to remember the correct order for scene headings if you note that the information progresses from general to specific.

The first dash eliminates the need for the word "ON", which is in a sense understood.

(C) EXT. JOHNSON HOUSE - DAY - (1979)

Any information having to do with time, year, season or hour of the day must appear in parentheses and be placed next to the specific element in the heading to which it applies.

The general rule of thumb is, if it falls at the end of the heading and on certain occasions or if there is more than one entry in parentheses, always place the information next to the specifics and never back to back, i.e., ( ) ( ).

(D) EXT. TENNESSEE STREET - (1992) - DAY - (5:00 PM)

Notice that the year entry (1992) is part of the location and works as a unit. It refers to a specific period of time in Tennessee. This information is then separated from the day with a dash, since DAY constitutes another element of time. Then, (5:00 pm) is part of the specific time period within the information.

(E) EXT./INT. JOHNSON'S HOUSE - DAY

The use of EXT./INT. means that two different but adjacent areas will be covered in the same scene. Only minimal camera movements will be required to proceed from one area to another. This means a character is first outside the house for a moment and then moves inside.

(F) JOANNE'S POV - SKY

This POV (Point of View) shot, tells us that we are seeing the sky through Joanne's eyes, which is the camera angle. There must always be a clear indication as to whose POV it is (the subject) and what the subject is looking at (the object).

(G) BACK TO SCENE

This tells us there was a short intervening scene which momentarily took us away from the original scene. The intervening scene is referred to as a *FLASHBACK*, which simply means a brief moment of time in the past and is in some way and somehow related to the present.

The time frame can differ depending on the circumstances. But for the most part, it is no longer than several moments. BACK TO SCENE is always capitalized and is most frequently used after a POV, INSERT or FLASHBACK to return to the original scene.

(H) TWO SHOT - JONES AND BROWN

Here both characters are exclusive subjects with little or no background details. Often this heading simply reads: JONES/BROWN.

(I) CLOSE-UP SHOT - JOANNE

In this scene, we see Joanne from the shoulders up. No background details are included or needed.

(J) ANGLE ON MS. HARRISON

This is a camera angle changing within a particular established area. It also works as a scene heading.

(K) EXTREME CLOSE-UP - JOANNE'S DIAMOND RING

As the term implies, this is a very close shot used to emphasize a specific object in detail. It is sometimes written incorrectly, i.e., ECU, or XCU. It should always be spelled out and in all capital letters and no abbreviations.

(L) MED/SHOT - JOANNE AND WILLIAM

This shot shows two characters from the waist up and may include some background details. Similar to TWO SHOT, MED means medium. This is the only camera angle which is abbreviated.

(M) EXT. MAGNUM P.I. - DAY - ESTABLISHING

Establishing here is a definite location and/or time of day. It may also be a STOCK shot that may already be on file in the film archives. This is mostly found in episodic TV.

An establishing shot can stand completely alone without any stage direction or dialogue. It serves as a quick point of reference as to where we are, at any given point of time in the story. The word STOCK refers to the entire heading. In this particular scene, it is available in the film archives and will need to be reshot. Most writers are in no position to know whether or not a given shot is in the archives unless the writer has written on a particular TV show or previous release.

(N) ANGLE ON DRIVER IN CONVERTIBLE - TRAVELING

This means this scene is being filmed as the car travels along a street. A second car with a camera mounted either on top, behind, along side or a second person inside the car films the action. A traveling shot is not to be confused with the camera cues. Camera cues are angles to determine what and how the viewer will see the characters and action and can also be used to emphasize one or more characters to set a mood or single out an object to give it additional importance.

DOLLY SHOT a k a TRAVELING, TRACKING, MOVING, or TRUCKING should appear in the direction, but may appear in the heading.

(O) ANGLE ON JOANNE AND WILLIAM - MOVING

DOLLY WITH THEM as they STROLL down the street talking EXCITEDLY.

When one or two characters are walking down the street and the camera is moving with them either, in front, behind or beside them, the scene should be stated to establish the character(s) with the camera cue DOLLY appearing in the direction. DOLLY may, on a rare occasion, appear as a heading reading DOLLY SHOT but more often than not appear only in the direction.

(P) INSERT - CLOCK ON THE WALL

An insert shot will usually depict a specific inanimate object such as: a newspaper, headline, a map, a photograph, a gun or some other object. Usually, it is accompanied by a short explanatory direction, but on rare occasions may stand alone. Whenever this heading appears, it is necessary to follow with the next shot going back to the original or previous scene. It is always placed at tab (19).

Example:

INSERT - CLOCK ON THE WALL

Time reads: TEN O'CLOCK P.M.

(Q) INTERCUT - JOANNE'S SUITE / WILLIAM'S - OFFICE - DAY

An INTERCUT is used to indicate two separate scenes simultaneously. It is often used with phone conversations to bring two specific locations together to form a scene. If both locations have been previously established, the INTERCUT is stated in the direction.

Example: Intercut used in direction.

INT. WILLIAM'S OFFICE - DAY

We SEE William on the telephone TALKING to Joanne in her suite.

INT. JOANNE'S SUITE - DAY

We SEE Joanne on the telephone and she is OBVIOUSLY excited by what she hears on the phone.

INTERCUT Joanne's reaction with William's conversation in his office.

(R) SERIES OF SHOTS

Example:

1. CAMERA FOLLOWS Chuck Norris RUNNING down a dark alley.

2. A CAR PULLS ACROSS and BLOCKS the exit of the alley.

3. Chuck OPENS the back door of the car and MOVES through as if caught in a Chinese fire drill.

This heading, as you can see, implies a series of short shots. These are usually action-types or mini-scenes which serve to move us quickly through time or a sequence of events. Chase scenes or highlights of a sporting event are usually written in this manner. Each shot is designated with a capital letter as shown above.

(S) MONTAGE

It is often confused with Series of Shots. Both concepts have come to be inter-changeable. A MONTAGE incorporates more on the screen simultaneously. At least two or more different but related subjects dissolve into and out of and/or into one another. A Montage is stated in the same manner as Series of Shots.

Example: MONTAGE

A) AERIAL SHOT - People RUNNING ramped through the streets.

B) People are running with arms FILLED with merchandise as they loot various stores.

C) National guard troops trying to restore order.

D) WIDE SHOT - Helicopters are flying over head.

Always capitalize all camera cues and scene headings; double space to separate each element. The major difference between a Series of Shots and a Montage is: a Series of Shots uses the principles, i.e., the major characters, and is filmed during the actual shooting of the film; a Montage is put together during post production or after the shooting and is done in the editing process.

SCENE ENDINGS

Scene endings are specific technical instructions indicating the method of moving from one scene to another. It is assumed that when moving from one to another, that we CUT TO: the next scene. Often, it's not necessary to use CUT TO. Although, it is the most commonly used. It should be used for a specific reason where there is no logical progression from one scene to another.

Example:

We are in California at a mansion party, we would then CUT TO: the bush camp in the Outback of Sidney, Australia. There are times when a more definitive instruction can be used to create a certain effect in moving from one scene to the next. You should use some endings sparingly and with a specific purpose in mind. Other endings which have specific technical directions are:

FADE TO:

FADE IN:

FADE OUT:

DISSOLVE TO:

MATCH TO:

MATCH CUT TO:

MATCH DISSOLVE TO:

CUT TO:

More Capitalizations

AD LIB'S, TITLES, NAMES, VOICE OVERS, BEGIN/END TITLES, FREEZE FRAMES.

(A) AD LIB calls for general, non-scripted conversation, laughter and the like among characters to serve as background atmosphere. The word AD LIB is the only word in the stage direction that must be capitalized.

Example:

We can HEAR AD LIB conversation in the small crowd, concerning the death of the chairman of the board.

(B) TITLES OF BOOKS, SONGS, OR MOVIES sometimes appear in direction and should always be capitalized and in *quotes*. Occasionally someone will request that the information appear in upper/lower case and quotes. This would be correct as well but should be used only when requested.

(C) VOICE OVER, when stated in direction, must be capitalized and spelled out. It is never abbreviated in stage direction, only in character direction.

Example:

MARY(O.S.)(V.O)

(D) BEGIN/END TITLES are always capitalized and may appear in direction. It is preferable to isolate these terms (double-spaced down) at the margin. In this way it is easy to see at a glance where the film titles should start and end.

(E) FREEZE FRAME works as a camera cue of sort. It tells the camera person to stop on a particular person and/or object and HOLD.

(F) NAMES in the character introduction and those with speaking roles must always be capitalized each time they are required to speak.

THE USE OF (V.O.) & (O.S.)

V.O. is for VOICE OVER, which means the character is not seen on the screen, but can be heard over some form of mechanical device, such as a telephone or a tape recorder, etc. A scene which requires narration is a (V.O.). We may hear a character thinking aloud or on a sound tape which is done during post production. While the camera might be on a character on the phone, we can hear the voice of the respondent on the other end, without ever seeing that other person. This is always a VOICE OVER situation.

SECTION FOUR SUMMARY

Paragraphing is used frequently in direction and should be obvious when it should occur. When using sound cues, it's important to be able to distinguish between actual and technical sounds. When using scene headings and endings, remember that there are two basic headings, INT. or EXT. However, there are shots that indicate more information found in the master scene. It's recommended that if you limit the use of numerous angles and shots, it will make it easier to read. Leave room for the director to use his skills to see things from several different angles. The endings are those basic endings used all the time. Voice Overs are basic technical terms used to distinguish that the character speaking is not visible on the screen. Off-screen refers to a character speaking who will become visible on the screen soon.

Notes:

Section Five

References

Abbreviations

Capitalizations

Punctuations

Samples:

  Scripts

  Treatments\Outlines

Glossary and Camera Terms

Index

References

This section was designed to bring together and provide a review of all the information and guidelines on abbreviations, capitalizations, and punctuations. It also gives you samples of the topics discussed in the previous sections.

Section Five

REFERENCES

Standard grammatical practices should be used when writing. However, there are exceptions when it comes to screenwriting. The following are a few of those exceptions along with technical usage of screenwriting terms.

ABBREVIATIONS

Abbreviations are used in scene headings/endings, stage direction, character cues, personal direction, sound cues, and camera cues.

Scene headings:

1)   INT.

2)   EXT.

Camera cues:

3)   MED. SHOT

4)   POV

Character cues:

5)   Personal Titles (also personal titles in personal direction)

6)   (V.O.)

7)   (O.S.)

8)   (O.C.)

Stage direction:

1)   Personal titles

2)   Other standard abbreviations

3)   b.g. - background

4)   f.g. - foreground

5)   O.S. - off screen

6)   O.C. - off camera

There are no abbreviations in scene endings. When the scene ending is too long to fit using tab (62), it must be backed off from the right margin (72), i.e., MATCH DISSOLVE TO.

CAPITALIZATIONS

1)   All words used in scene headings, scene endings and personal titles should be capitalized.

2)   Character instructions and directions or any words used for emphasis.

3)   Songs, books, movie titles

4)   AD LIB'S

5)   VOICE OVERS, except in character direction

6)   O.S. - off screen

7)   O.C. - off camera

PUNCTUATIONS

1) Dashes are used to separate elements in scene headings.

2) Parenthesis are used to denote time of day, season and year. Parenthesis are also used in character direction, and character cues and specific role designations after character name, i.e., (DR.), (SGT.), etc.

3) Quotes around books, songs and movie titles.

4) Semicolon between continuing or beat and additional direction.

5) Colons are always used at the end of scene headings and scene endings, with the exception of FADE OUT, which constitutes the end of the script.

Sample Scripts / Treatment and Outlines Only

The following examples and samples cannot be copied, reproduced or in any way be altered and used without written permission.

Sample Script for Feature Film

<u>THE LAST PICASSO</u>

FADE IN:

EXT. BEVERLY HILLS CALIFORNIA - DAY - WIDESHOT - (SUPER IMPOSE - 1992

Its an incredibly clear sunny summers afternoon, as we PAN the SKYLINE, OVER-LOOKING the magnificent Mansions, with their well-manicured lawns.

We ZOOM IN on one SPECIFIC Mansion, where we SEE several small groups of people STANDING around the CIRCULAR driveway, dressed in black

We HEAR AD LIB conversation, concerning the recent death of one of the mansions former occupants.

ANGLE ON DRIVEWAY ENTRANCE

We SEE a Black Rolls Royce Limousine ENTER and we FOLLOW as it makes its way UP the circular drive and come to rest in a space marked "Reserved", and we SEE the Driver LEAP from the front door and OPEN the rear door and its occupant EXITS.

CLOSE ANGLE ON JEREMY BRECKENRIDGE

A well-groomed, handsome, well-tanned man in his late thirties, about six-feet-three inches in height and in excellent physical condition.

We FOLLOW as he makes his way through the crowd of mourners and well-wishers, toward the entrance to the mansion. His every step, exudes, self-confidence and aggressiveness, but can be sensitive and compassionate. If he feels threatened or challenged, he will stop at nothing to thwart his opposition.

                                                    CUT TO:

INT. MANSION - STUDY - DAY - ON FUNERAL PROGRAM

As it is being PICKED UP from the desk and the CAMERA ADJUSTS to include Jeremy as he ENTERS the room from the

foyer, closing the door behind. We cannot see who's holding
the program, we can only HEAR a MAN'S VOICE.

                         (V.O.) (O.S.)
                    Well Jeremy...have you made
                    your choice as to your father's
                    successor?
                         (beat)
                    Considering the only logical
                    choice is rather an obvious
                    one!

                         JEREMY
                         (removes his coat)
                    To be honest with you.-- After
                    reviewing the credentials of
                    all the potential candidates --
                    and mind you there were a few
                    extremely qualified.
                         (beat)
                    I couldn't make a fair decision
                    and be totally impartial
                    without being bias.
                         (moving to his desk)
                    So I decided the best person to
                    succeed my father is ME!

CLOSE ANGLE ON HOWARD JONES

A somewhat staunch-looking older gentlemen, business type,
late sixties. A man from the old school. He believes in
equal rights for all, as long as it doesn't infringe on his
rights to believe in total white supremacy. With that
announcement, he becomes a bit put out and irritated by
Jeremy's statement.

                         HOWARD
                         (frustration in voice)
                    Young man! ... What the hell do
                    you know about the management
                    of a multi-billion dollar
                    corporation. --Your sitting in
                    on an occasional board meeting
                    does not a chairman make!
                         (crushing program in
                         hand)

3

It takes a hell-of-a-lot more
than a passing fancy and the
make a wish foundation to
properly head a corporation.

Howard begins PACING back and forth, in front of Jeremy's
desk and we HEAR the FRUSTRATION in his voice RISE to a
FEVERED PITCH.

                    HOWARD
                  (continues)
          And frankly sonny boy -- I
          don't think you have the balls
          for such a monumental under-
          taking.

                    JEREMY
          It's rather interesting that
          when you and my father signed
          the partnership agreement over
          thirty years ago, you swore up
          and down, that the author of
          the agreement was a genius. ...
          Then, when you heard who the
          architect/genius was ...
                  (pointing to himself)
          You said, and I quote, "If it
          ever came down to naming a
          successor and I decided to
          succeed my father as chairman,
          you would put your vote of
          confidence and support behind
          me"!
                  (beat)
          What happened, ... a change of
          mind?

                    HOWARD
          Things, circumstances and
          people do on occasion.
                  (beat)
          But, taking into account, I do
          own forty-percent stock in this
          company, which gives me auto-
          matic ...

                    JEREMY
                (interrupts)
        Yeah!-- And, I own the
        remainder, Remember! ...

Jeremy STANDS UP behind his desk and WALKS around to the
front to confront Howard face to face.

                    JEREMY
                (continuing)
        Listen! ... It wasn't enough
        that during my father's term-
        inal illness, which took his
        life, that you constantly
        badgered the HELL out of him to
        name you as his successor!...
                (beat)
        But, every time you got a D...N
        opportunity that presented you
        a forum to vent your
        frustrations and views of
        displeasure, you pounced on it
        like some "Dog in Heat"!
                (puts finger in
                 Howard's chest)
        And frankly, I am about fed up
        with your penny ante "BULL
        CRAP"! ...

                    HOWARD
        It's obvious, we will not be
        able to settle this issue, so
        we'll let the board of
        director's make their choice
        and I can tell you this.
                (beat)
        I'll see you dead and in hell,
        before I'll let you take over
        this company!

Jeremy begins BACKING Howard from the room, POKING his
finger in Howard's chest.

                         JEREMY
                    (angered)
              Are you threatening my life?
                    (beat)
              If you think you will be
              selected as chairman, then I
              will see you in hell!

Jeremy OPENS the door and SHOVES Howard from the room and
SLAMS the door in his face

                                        CUT TO:

EXT. FEDERATED ACCOUNTANTS INC. - MEMPHIS TENN. - EVENING -
(5:00PM)

AND SO-ON AND SO-ON ----------------------

SAMPLE SCRIPT FOR TELEVISION SITCOM

<u>THE LAST PICASSO</u>

<u>ACT ONE</u>

FADE IN:

<u>EXT. BEVERLY HILLS CALIFORNIA-DAY</u>
<u>WIDESHOT</u>
(JEREMY BRECKENRIDGE
HOWARD JONES)

ITS AN INCREDIBLY CLEAR SUNNY SUMMER
AFTERNOON, AS WE PAN THE GROUNDS OF
THIS MANSION TO SEE SEVERAL SMALL
GROUPS OF PEOPLE, STANDING AROUND,
DRESSED IN BLACK.

WE HEAR AD LIB CONVERSATION,
CONCERNING THE RECENT DEATH OF ONE
OF THE FORMER MANSION RESIDENTS.

ANGLE JEREMY MICHAEL BRECKENRIDGE

WE PICKUP AND FOLLOW A WELL-GROOMED,
HANDSOME, TANNED MAN, IN HIS LATE
THIRTIES, EARLY FORTIES, ABOUT SIX-
FEET FOUR INCHES IN HEIGHT AND IN
EXCELLENT HEALTH.

WE FOLLOW HIM AS HE MAKES HIS WAY
THROUGH THE CROWD OF MOURNERS AND
WELL-WISHERS, TOWARD THE FRONT DOOR
OF THE MANSION.

CUT TO:

INT. MANSION - FOYER/STUDY - ON
FUNERAL PROGRAM

WE SEE THE FRONT DOOR OPEN AND
PICKUP JEREMY AS HE ENTERS AND IS
GREETED BY THE BUTLER.

                    BUTLER

     You have a visitor in the study

     sir.

(TAKES JEREMY'S COAT)

                    JEREMY

     Who is it?

                    BUTLER

     Mr. Jones sir!

                    JEREMY

     Oh shoot!--Not that son-of-a-gun!

(BEAT)

     I'll have a seven and seven in

     about ten minutes.

                    BUTLER

     Very good sir!

(BEAT)

     Will there be anything for your

     guest sir?

                    JEREMY

     He won't be here long enough to

     have a paper cup of piss...if I

     can help it!

WE FOLLOW JEREMY TOWARD THE DOOR

INT. STUDY - ON FUNERAL PROGRAM - ON
DESK

AS IT'S BEING PICKED UP FROM THE
DESK AND THE CAMERA ADJUSTS AS THE
DOOR OPENS AND TO SEE JEREMY ENTER
THE ROOM, CLOSING THE DOOR BEHIND.

WE CAN'T SEE WHO'S HOLDING THE
PROGRAM, WE CAN ONLY HEAR A MAN'S
VOICE.

> (V.O.) (O.S.)
>
> Well!...Have you made a decision
>
> as to your father's successor?

(BEAT)

> Considering the only logical
>
> choice is rather evident!

> JEREMY
>
> Honestly,--I have and you weren't
>
> considered one of my choices.

> HOWARD
>
> What the heck do you mean, I'm not
>
> one of those considered?

(BEAT)

> HOWARD(CONTD)

(FRUSTRATION IN VOICE)

> You must have forgotten, I own
>
> forty-percent of this company!

                        JEREMY

        NO! I hadn't forgotten, but you

        must have forgotten, that now that

        my father is dead, I own the

        remaining sixty percent, which

        gives me control!

WE SEE THE ANGER AND FRUSTRATION ON
HOWARD'S FACE AS HE CRUMPLES THE
PROGRAM IN HIS HAND.

                                    CUT TO:

            END OF ACT ONE

ACT TWO

FADE IN:

INT. PRIVATE OFFICE - DAY
(JERI JACOBS, PERRY SAMUELS)

WE SEE AN EXTREMELY ATTRACTIVE WOMAN
SEATED AT HER DESK WORKING AT THE
COMPUTER.

THE EXPRESSION ON HER FACE IS ONE OF
INTENSE CONCENTRATION AND WE HEAR A
KNOCK ON HER DOOR, BREAKING HER
CONCENTRATION.

                    JERI

        SHOOT!... Who the heck is it now?

    (BEAT)

            COME IN!

THE CAMERA PANS TO THE DOOR TO SEE A
MAN ENTER.

ANGLE ON PERRY SAMUELS

A YOUNG MAN, EARLY TWENTIES, DRESSED
IN (G.M. DESIGNERS)= GOODWILL.

HE APPROACHES AND TAKES A SEAT IN
FRONT OF JERI'S DESK WITHOUT BEING
ASKED.

                    SAMUELS

(HEAVY SOUTHERN ACCENT)

        Didn't chu git my memo?

                    JERI

     I may have, but I don't recall

     reading it at this time.

(BEAT)

     Why?

SAMPLE SCRIPT FOR SOAPS
- STUDIO

<u>END OF ACT II</u>

<u>JEREMY AND HOWARD'S
CONFRONTATION IN THE STUDY
OVER CHAIRMANSHIP AND
CONTROL</u>

<u>TEASER</u>

FADE IN:

INT. MANSION - STUDY

WE SEE JEREMY SEATED AT HIS DESK AND
HOWARD STANDING IN FRONT.

HOWARD IS HOLDING A PIECE OF PAPER
IN HIS RIGHT HAND AND SUDDENLY
CRUMPLES IT.

                    JEREMY

You seem to be a bit upset,

over the fact that I'm going

to replace my father as

chairman.

                    HOWARD

You darn right, I'm upset. I

should be pissed off, but

I'm trying to get you to

reconsider and recommend me
as the obvious successor.

JEREMY

Now, why would I do such an
idiotic thing, after what
you put my father through
and the malicious attacks
against me over whether or
not I should be the
successor.

(BEAT)

There's no way in hell I
will support a person with
the racist point or view you
have.

WE SEE THE ANGER COME TO HOWARD'S
FACE AS WE

DISSOLVE TO:

1

FADE IN:

JERI JACOBS AND PERRY SAMUEL'S
OFFICE

Sample Treatments/Outlines

GREATEST LOVE

The year is 1953, St. Joseph's Hospital, Memphis, Tennessee. A rather unique set of siblings have just been born on this very stormy night in July.

Jeremy M. and Jeri M. Breckenridge

The pair is not your normal siblings, due to their parentage combinations. They are separated at birth due to the circumstances surrounding their parents. Medical problems of Jeri and the death of her mother forces the state to place her in an orphanage.

A few months later, Jeremy's mother dies from pneumonia and the father is left with the task of trying to raise a son. Poverty and mounting hospital bills further push him toward the only source of comfort available at the time, alcohol, which further complicates matters. The father's alcohol problems force the state department to remove Jeremy and place him in the same orphanage.

After a few years of sobriety, the state allows their father to retrieve his son after being advised that his daughter had been adopted earlier and that her whereabouts are unknown.

With his son Jeremy in tow, the father Mr. Breckenridge relocates to Los Angeles, California, where he builds a multi-billion dollar investment banking empire.

The year is 1992, the elder Breckenridge has died and Jeremy is destined to succeed his father as chairman and sole heir to the multi-billion dollar empire. He is confronted by Howard Jones, stockholder and owner of 40% of the corporation. Jones feels he should be the next chairman, but Jeremy has ideas of his own.

While working late one night at the office, Jeremy makes a startling discovery, as he prepares for his first board meeting. The discovery is the possibility of a sibling who has been given one half of his inheritance. This further complicates his life. Jeremy has to make a decision as to whether or not to divulge this information to the board or keep it to himself, hoping no one finds out. Unknown to him, there's a spy watching his every move. Before Jeremy has an opportunity to make a decision, Howard reveals the information in an attempt to discredit Jeremy.
The vice-chairman, Kelvin Nelson, offers Jeremy an opportunity to prove his leadership ability by completing the acquisition of a company, in which his father had began, prior to his death. Jeremy accepts the challenge but must face the reality that even if he's successful and voted in as chairman, he still could lose controlling interest, unless he's able to find and convince his sibling to support him.

Unknown to Jeremy, the company which he must acquire is the one that his sibling is employed as Asst. Finance Dir. Jeri Jacobs, an extremely attractive woman, whose intelligence far surpasses her obvious fashion model beauty. Jeri is confronted by her new superior to reduce her already small staff by an additional 75%, 85% being blacks. Jeri refuses his request due to his obvious racist attitude, putting her career in jeopardy. The chairman of the company, Clarence Jamerison, a man who would sell his own mother for a dollar, offers Jeri an opportunity to represent them as the senior financial advisor and full partnership after the acquisition is completed.

She accepts the promotion, in hopes of finally getting the long-overdue partner status she's wanted. She's unaware of the plot to terminate her once the acquisition is complete.

Jeremy and Jeri's first meeting isn't the usual. Jeremy is put off with the idea of working with a subordinate, but his assistant Ronald convinces him to at least give her a chance. Jeremy, reluctantly agrees.

Jeremy begins searching for his sibling by going back to the now abandoned orphanage. No luck there — so he's taken to a local blues bar by a cabby and is pulled into a family feud, resulting in a barroom brawl.

Jeri takes Jeremy on a tour of the offices and they discuss various topics. During their discussion, both make statements that unknown to them will be put to the test in the very near future.

Jeri uncovers information of a possible conspiracy and tries to confront those possibly involved. He is forbidden to confront them and is removed from the meeting. In frustration, she leaves and is involved in an almost fatal car crash.

While Jeremy and Ronald are having at dinner in the hotel's restaurant, Jeremy is wounded during a bundled robbery attempt. While recovering at the hotel, a hotel employee overhears Jeremy and Ronald in a heated verbal exchange, just before Ronald gives him a package revealing the possible conspiracy.

Before Jeremy has an opportunity to investigate any further, he receives an unusual request, to become a marrow donor to a stranger. He learns that Jeri is the recipient and is moved with compassion.

While Jeremy is recovering after surgery, an attempt is made on his life. Unknown to Ronald, he will be accused of attempted murder and arrested. After Ronald is cleared , Jeremy and Ronald receive assistance from another attorney. Time is running out to complete the acquisition. Jeremy has to abandon his search and concentrate on the acquisition.

Jeremy thwarts the conspiracy and successfully completes the deal and returns to Los Angeles, only to learn that Howard has sold his interest in the corporation to a Japanese investment firm. And, there's nothing he can do to prevent it. With 30% of outstanding stock up in the air, there seems to be no way for Jeremy to raise the needed capital in time. The investors have made a bid to acquire them also.

While Jeri's at home recuperating from the surgery, she receives a visit from her high school guidance counselor just as a news bulletin flashes on the TV screen. Jeremy announces his impending doom. The counselor advises Jeri of Jeremy's visit. Jeri begins to put two and two together along with information given her by the doctor and things begin to fit. She realizes the possible connection between her and Jeremy.

Jeremy stands before the board of directors about to concede to Howard, when Jeri interrupts the meeting to confront Jeremy face to face. She reveals her identity with matching proof. Howard forgot the general partnership clause, preventing the sale or distribution of any said shares, without approval by the general partner. Failure to do so would result in the automatic loss of said shares which would revert back to the general partner.

Howard loses his stock.   Jeremy and Jeri own 100% of the stock. They live happily ever after as brother and sister.

Jeremy throws a dinner party and welcomes his sister home.

Sample Treatments/Outlines

PREMIUM

The oftentimes failures and successes of Premium, a small American town trying to survive in this age of wealth and opportunity and the few dedicated citizens who try to make it happen.

In the early 70's, Premium was a thriving, prosperous and fully employed town boasting a population of 52,350 citizens. Today, that number has shrunk to 40,000. The unemployed and their families have left via the highway running through Premium to Los Angeles and parts unknown, to find employment again.

Premium's two major contributors to prosperity and health plans are Roller Ball Ball Bearings and Fancy Pants. But, as inflation suffocates the nation, Roller Ball and Fancy Pants pull out and relocate to Mexico where they find cheap labor.

Thereafter, most of Premium's citizenry boycotts Fancy Pants' products. Women burn bras and undergarments. Men, confiscate shinny steel marbles from their sons.

Except for a few dedicated citizens like Officer Hiram J. Moosehead, Judge I.B. Racist and Elimay Sue Jones, Premium would have become just another ghost town. To them, Premium is what America is all about, a town with a heart, a land where dreams of a good life are still possible.

PLOT EPISODE:

Premium Paper Products, the last large manufacturing plant in
town employs over one thousand workers and supplies the Burger
King's chains with toilet paper and napkins. Rumors are spread-
ing they are planning to move out of Premium. Their departure,
if not prevented will surely bankrupt the city and make Premium
another ghost town on America's planes and nobody wants to see
that happen. When Officer Moosehead goes to the bank to cash his
weekly pay check, it bounces. Suspecting that the city's coffers
are about bankrupt, Hiram decides upon a desperate measure to
bring in a few extra bucks. If you are into frozen delights for
the microwave, shop at Johnny's. Hiram's last hope is Elimay Sue,
a true-blue Premiumite. Elimay is the postmaster and was the
director of the unemployment office, when there was unemployment.
But there are no long lines—benefits have run out.

Elimay's husband, Timothy, left Premium with Roller Ball when
they shipped out to Mexico and hasn't been heard of since.
Elimay's correspondence has always been returned, "NO FORWARDING
ADDRESS/RETURN TO SENDER"

Only sheer dedication brings Hiram to ask for help. He knows
better.

Below is a review of major questions to ask yourself about your script and character functions. Be brutal in your responses.

A) Do you have a confidante(s)? If so, are they overly talky, or have you found ways to reveal and show rather than tell?

B) Do you have several characters with the same functions? If so, cut or combine characters.

C) Are you missing a function? Perhaps you need another catalyst figure, or your reader will have trouble understanding the theme without a thematic character.

D) Is your protagonist (hero) receiving help along the way from supporting characters? Are they really supporting your character or just hanging around?

E) As the writer, do you have a character who carries your personal point of view? If so, have you kept the character active and dramatic rather than talky? Does your point-of-view give insight to the story, or is it simply a message you have been trying to get across and thought you'd sneak it in now?

F) Are you dealing with subject matter which is not believable to the masses? If so, have you created at least one point of view character to help suspend their disbelief, at least for the course of the film?

G) Are you dealing with material open to misinterpretation? If so, have you included at least one balanced character to protect yourself?

H) Do you have humor in your film? Does one character carry the comic relief? Do you use it to release tension or to lighten up the material?

I) Count the number of characters that are taking focus throughout the story? If you need to, identify and keep track of more than seven. There may be too many and you will need to find places to cut in order that the reader can easily follow the story and the various characters through lines.

J)   Who are my supporting characters and do they contribute to the story or are they merely "message" carriers?

There have been numerous films which have failed at the box office because there were too many characters without a clear story function. Scripts should be clean, clear and easy to follow. Every character must have a function to perform and each must have a reason to be in your story.

GLOSSARY AND COMMON CAMERA TERMS

"A" Page A term used to describe additional pages added to a script. The page number is used along with A.B.C. etc. to keep the pages consecutive.

Above The Line A film's BUDGET is divided into two main sections: Above the line and Below the line. ATL *abbrev.* expenditures are usually negotiated on a RUN OF SHOW basis and generally are the most expensive individual items on the budget, e.g., cost for story and screenplay, producer, director and cast).

Above The Title This refers to the position of FRONT CREDITS that appear before the main title of the film. The order of credits is usually as follows: Distributor, Producer/ Production Co., that presents a (name of Director) film, followed by name(s) of principal star(s) then the film title.

Accelerated Motion Action shot with the camera running at a speed of less than 24 frames per second (normal sound speed) so that when projected at normal speed, it appears speeded-up.

A.C.E. Abbrev. for American Cinema Editors. An honorary professional society of film editors. Membership is by invitation only.

Action The cause and effect relationship. It's what happens in a screenplay caused by characters interacting and the changes which tells the story. It is also what the Director says when he/she wishes the movement /dialogue in a scene to commence.

Action Still A photograph blown up from an actual frame of a motion picture taken during production with a still camera.

Action Track The film (picture) before any music, dialogue or effects tracks are added.

AD. Abbrev. Assistant Director.

Adaptation A screenplay whose story comes from another medium, such as: a novel, short story, magazine or newspaper article, etc.

Added Scene An additional scene inserted into a script that has already been assigned Scene numbers. The added scene is noted with a letter beside the number.

AD LIB Extemporaneous lines or phrases appropriate to a given situation. Example: AD LIB greetings when guest arrive at a party. (Off the cuff), generally not written in the script and just made up as one goes along.

ADR. Abbrev. for Automatic Dialogue Replacement.

Advance The number of frames by which the sound recording must precede the film Image in order to be in SYNC. For 35 mm, the advance is 20 frames and 16 mm, 26 frames.

Aerial Shot The camera is airborne, shooting from airplane or helicopter.

Air to Air Used to describe a shot of a flying object taken from another flying object, such as a helicopter or plane.

Ambience Mood, feeling or presence that is the desired effect in a scene.

111

Ambient Sound Normal sounds that exist in a particular place (e.g., street noises, chirping birds, wind, room tone)

Angle Favoring The camera is aimed primarily at a specific character or object.

Antagonist The villain, the character whose main objective is to prevent the hero from getting to the truth, thereby creating the main conflict.

Answer Print The first composite (sound and picture) print that the lab sends for approval.

Apple Box The standard size wooden crate used to raise the height of people, lights, props, etc., during shooting.

Arranger The person who prepares and adapts previously written music for presentation in some form other than its original form.

Art Department The crew members who, under direction of the production designer, are responsible for creating the look of a film as far as SETS and LOCATIONS are concerned. This staff usually includes the Art Director, an Asst. Art Dir., Costume Designer, Set Designer, Draftsmen and Apprentice.

Art Director The person responsible for every aspect of the films decor and set construction. He must be knowledgeable in architecture, design, etc.

Assembly The first step of editing when scenes are put together in script sequence, to roughly tell the story.

Audio Anything related to the sound portion of the film or tape, as opposed to the video or visual portion.

Baby Legs. (a k a Shorty) A short camera stand (tripod) used for shooting low angles. Its the smallest of the three tripods.

Backers Audition The showing of a film in a workshop setting, presented specifically for an audience of potential backers.

b.g. (BACKGROUND) An activity or sound in a scene that is secondary or subordinate to the main action and serves as a backdrop for the action. Used in direction and always abbreviated in lower case followed by a period after each letter.

Background Noises Sounds that give the illusion of action OFF-CAMERA or general ambience (e.g., car honk, muffled voices, a train whistle frogs croaking etc.) These sounds are added to the sound track in post production.

Backdrop A painted or photographic rendering used to give the illusion of a real Background, such as a view through a door or window, or natural setting on a interior SET.

Backlight A technique of lighting a subject from behind, relative to camera position, creating a silhouette or halo effect.

Back Lot An open-air part of a Studio where Exteriors may be shot. There are many different standing sets and studios that save a great deal of money by not having to build new elaborate sets.

Back-Up Schedule (a k a Cover Set) An alternate film location and timetable which can be used in the event that shooting cannot proceed as planned, such as: bad weather etc.

Baffle A sound absorbing screen inside a loudspeaker which improves fidelity by increasing or decreasing reverberation.

Bank.(a k a Coops) A large number of lamps mounted in a single housing, used for illuminating large areas.

Barn Doors Folding metal gates on lamps that help direct and control the light.

Battery Belt A compact, portable energy source worn by the camera operator around their waist, plugged into the camera, thus giving the operator maximum mobility.

Bazooka A studio light support for use on a catwalk.

Beat Sheet Writer's term for a page or two containing one or two-line summaries of stories. Usually used in episodic or serial television.

Belly Board A small platform for mounting a camera as close to ground level as possible.

Best Boy Two separate positions: second in command to the Gaffer and to the Key Grip. The Best boy/Grip is in charge of the rest of the grips and grip equipment; the best boy / electric is in charge of the rest of the electricians and equipment.

Bible Run The complete, updated weekly accounting of all activity on a motion picture production, computerized.

Billing The placement of names, titles etc., in the credits. In addition to salary and points in a film, billing is a major issue when negotiating a deal.

Blacks Cloths or Drapes used to block daylight from windows or doorways when shooting night interiors or to create the illusions of night when shooting a small, night exterior. An interesting exception: large portions of Universal Studio's back lot were blacked out when shooting Streets of Fire as it was less expensive than shooting night for night.

Blanks Ammunition that contains paper or plastic in place of the bullet.

Blocking Laying out the action or movement in a scene with the actors and/or camera.

Bloom Treatment of any glass surface, excluding the camera lens with a special transparent fluoride to reduce glare.

Blue Pages Added pages and changes that are put into an already numbered script once the script have been distributed on a production.

Blue Screen Shot A delicate and elaborate special effects process whereby the subject is filmed in front of a special, monochromatic blue background with normal film. Blue sensitive mattes are made to replace the blue background with other footage. When combined, the subject and background look as if they were shot simultaneously. The bicycle flying scene in *ET* was shot in this manner.

Boom A counterbalanced extension device which allows a camera or microphone to follow the action in a fluid continuous movement.

Boom Shot (a k a crane shot) A continuous shot incorporating a number of different camera angles from different levels, usually accomplished with the use of a crane.

113

Breakaway Props that are specially designed to fall or break apart on impact such as: bottles, chairs, windows etc.

Breakdown Prepared by the production manager or assist director, it is an extremely detailed system of separating each and every element in the script and then rearranging them in the most effective and least expensive manner for filming.

Burn-In To lay white titles, usually captions or subtitles over the picture in order to identify a person, place or thing, or to translate dialogue. (a k a SUPER IMPOSE)

Business Any small movement or action used by an actor in a scene to further the action and/or add color to the interpretation of his/her character.

Bus To As opposed to report to, this signifies a location day for the crew. Their work (pay) time begins with the bus ride to the location and ends when they are dropped off after the completion of the day's work.

Button A television term for a dramatic or comedic punch or topper at the end of a scene.

Climax The highest point of the film, in which we should see the principle character(s) dealing with the consequences of their actions.

Close Shot A camera shot involving just the shoulders and head of a character. Not to be confused with CLOSE-UP. Always spelled out and capitalized.

Close-Up A camera shot that closely examines and/or emphasizes some extreme details either on a person or inanimate object. Incorrectly used abbreviated but correctly spelled out and capitalized.

Collaboration Working cooperatively with someone else on a creative project.

Combination Page A page which is assigned two or more consecutive numbers to account for pages that have been deleted from the script as a result of editing.

Condensing Cheating on spacing to make a screenplay type out to fewer pages and does not reflect an accurate page count.

Crane Shot The camera is mounted on a mobile arm, i.e., a boom and swings through the air in any appropriate direction.

Crisis The highest point of tension in a screenplay just before the climax in which the most important issues hang in the balance. The crisis is broken by the main character deciding to do something.

Critique To evaluate and look critically and analytically at a creative work, weighing it's strong and weak points.

Development The unfolding of the plotline through actions by the characters that cause new things to happen, which in turn causes the main character to move in new directions. It is also known as the way a screenplay is structured, building from beginning to end.

Dialogue The words spoken by the characters in your story.

Dissolve To A scene ending used to indicate that a particular scene should gradually fade away.

Dollies A camera cue used in direction instructing the camera to move along with the subject(s) of the scene. This is achieved by using either a hand held or secured to an apparatus camera on wheels. It is always in cap's in direction.

Draft A version of a completed screenplay/script that needs testing, rewriting and polishing.

Ellipsis/Dashes The ellipsis is a series of (. . .) periods used to signify a pause or change in sequences. Use of the ellipsis or dashes(-), often indicates that a word(s) have been left out because they are usually "understood".

Establishing Shot It tells you where you are, i.e., the location. A shot of the Eiffel Tower establishes Paris. It is mostly used in the very beginning of the story.

Exposition The opening of the screenplay in which we learn the important background information for the events that will follow.

EXT. (EXTERIOR) Indicates that a particular scene takes place outdoors. Used in scene headings, always abbreviated, followed by a period and capitalized.

EXTREME CLOSE UP The camera is in very close, usually on an object for the purpose of spotlighting detail. Can also be used to accentuate a specific character's facial expression. Often combined with ZOOM IN: Do not abbreviate. It is always spelled out and capitalized.

EXTREME LONG-SHOT A scene ending that involves shooting an "all encompassing" scene from a considerable distance away. Do not abbreviate. Spell out and capitalize.

FADE IN The term used to begin the story and script.

FADE OUT A scene ending used at the end of a scene or act and at the end of the film. It should not appear in the middle of a script (without acts) since FADE TO: is the correct term to use. FADE OUT: means that the scene or film is over and will gradually darken and fade to black. The end.

Film Format The specific script format used for a one camera production. A term used interchangeably with screenplay, one camera and feature film formats.

f.g. (Foreground) Those activities which take place nearest the viewer in perspective. Focus here may also be an object. Opposite of background. Used in direction and the same as in b.g..

Freeze Frame Works as a camera direction rather than a scene ending. It means that the picture stops moving and holds on a specific fact. It can be a clock, diamond ring or calendar etc.

FULL SHOT Taking in most of the set or scene, as a wide-angle shot inside a specific location.

HIGH ANGLE SHOT Camera looks down on a scene or person.

INSERT A scene involving an inanimate object which gives us a certain piece of information or calls our attention to a specific fact. It can be a clock, diamond ring or calendar, etc.

INT. (INTERIOR) Indicates that a particular scene will be shot indoors. Just the opposite of EXT.

115

LONG SHOT A camera angle shot from some distance, including considerable background details. Capitalized and spelled out.

LOCATION The place in which a scene occurs and is shot, i.e., the living room of a house, a beach, cabin of an airplane etc.

LOW ANGLE SHOT The complete opposite of high angle shot.

MASTER SCENE Usually, "major scenes" which designate a location where several shots/angles may take place. Begins with EXT. or INT.

MATCH CUT Involves matching the subject of one scene to the next scene. EXAMPLE: We SEE a unique brooch being worn at a dinner party in one scene and then, we MATCH CUT: to SEE the same brooch in the next scene, in a pawn shop window.

MEDIUM SHOT A shot of one or two characters from the MED. SHOT waist up. The only camera angle that is abbreviated. Always capitalize.

MONTAGE Two or more related subjects on the screen at the same time blended in a montage effect. It's a scene heading. The end of a montage must be indicated in capital letters and isolated at the direction margin. (END OF MONTAGE)

M.O.S. Without sound.

Motivation The reason behind a character's action. What makes them react in the manner they do.

MOVING SHOT A camera cue used in direction to indicate that the camera should move with the subject(s) being filmed.

O.C. (OFF-CAMERA) Sounds or dialogue heard while the camera is on another subject. It is the same as Off-Screen, however, Off-Camera is the term used in three camera television formats. Always capitalized, abbreviated and followed by periods after each letter and in parenthesis.

O.S. (OFF-SCREEN) Term used in screenplays and one camera film formats. A character talks from an adjacent area, such as a room or somewhere else other than in view of the camera. Sounds may also be (O.S./ capitalized, abbreviate, same as O.C.

PAN The camera moves slowly from left to right or vise versa, not stopping on any one thing or person until instructed to do so by use of the terms PICK UP:, etc.

Plot The key events that happen to character(s) in a story.

POV (POINT OF VIEW) The viewpoint of a character(s). When the audience sees something through the eyes of the person and sees what they see. Always capitalized and abbreviated.

Props Abbreviated for properties. These are any objects used by a character in their performance. Anything which is part of the set, such as a water pitcher, deck of cards, or a paper clip on a desk etc.

Protagonist The main character or "hero", whom the story is built around.

PICK-UP The camera is moving in any way and stops on a certain person or object.

Reverse POV A point of view shot turned 180 degrees to show the original subject.

Resolution The ending of the screenplay, after the climax. Here, we see how the character(s) are going to handle the events that just happened to them.

Run Several pages in consecutive sequence. Used with references to revision pages.

Set-up A camera position or camera angle.

Scene A division of the screenplay that occurs in one specific location during filming when something happens to move the story along.

Script The written version of the story. It tells the setting, what words will be said, the character's state of mind and a brief statement of the action.

Secondary Characters The character(s) in a story with whom the main character is principally involved with or whom the main character cares about most. The main character's relationship with the secondary is usually complicated by the antagonist, also known as "supporting characters".

SERIES OF SHOTS A series of short action sequences which serve to move the film quickly through time, experience or stream of consciousness.

Simultaneous Dialogue Two characters speaking at the same time. Dialogue may be placed side by side on the page. Tabs are not necessary to accommodate this situation, because it's a rare occasion.

Sitcom A shortened term meaning, situation comedy, used for television only.

Shooting Schedule A day by day schedule of filming set up for a production staff.

SFX. (SOUND EFFECTS) Used in tape formats for television and film. It requires technical reproduction of a sound usually dubbed onto the sound track. Windblowing, laser guns firing etc. Abbreviated and capitalized.

SFEX. (SPECIAL EFFECTS) Also used in formats for television and film. It requires the same as SFX, except for such things as: smoke billowing from under a door and the like.

Split Screen One or more subjects on the screen simultaneously, but in different locations and the screen is split in half.

Stage Direction Gives the character(s) a direction in which to move and action to take at a given period of time.

STOCK Scenes you don't have to shoot, but can be ready-made from the film archives.

SLOW MOTION The action is artificially slowed down, during post production/editing.

Index